# 9/11
# DECODED

# 9/11 DECODED

## JOURNEY TO POLYNESIA

JIM GARRITY

iUniverse®

**9/11 DECODED**
**JOURNEY TO POLYNESIA**

*iUniverse books may be ordered through booksellers or by contacting:*

*iUniverse*
*1663 Liberty Drive*
*Bloomington, IN 47403*
*www.iuniverse.com*
*1-800-Authors (1-800-288-4677)*

*ISBN: 978-1-4917-7890-6 (sc)*
*ISBN: 978-1-4917-7966-8 (hc)*
*ISBN: 978-1-4917-7889-0 (e)*

*Library of Congress Control Number: 2015953744*

*Print information available on the last page.*

*iUniverse rev. date: 10/12/2015*

# DEDICATIONS

This book is dedicated to that lovely and inspiring lady - Mary Wilson of the Supremes who has visited Laos, which received a $3 million grant from the U.S. Department of Agriculture to improve the quality of life of children who were not attending school because they were hungry or in danger of unexploded ordnances. While in Muangkhai Village, Laos, Ms. Wilson began the discharge of more than two tons of explosives found in and around villages and schools. Her plans included travel to Vietnam, Cambodia and Okinawa, as well as returning to Laos, to clear landmines still active from the Vietnam War, which ended more than four decades ago. I like her rendition of 'Fields of Gold' so it is a ballad theme for this book.

Also

In Memory of my son Duncan who died at birth and to Mum, Dad and Sisters Kathleen and Rosemary.

This book is also dedicated to loved ones counting friends and family.

And to all the staff at iUniverse in the Philippines and the USA for without all their kind help and guidance this book would not be possible.

# *Preface*

The narrator tells a story, within this historical account, of his disaffection with the neoconservatives who have steadily gained inroads into the Republican Party in recent decades. They were in top positions and had a powerful influence over the new President in 2001.

The narrator believes in strong, accountable government and self-determination; a Government that would protect the Bill of Rights instead of passing laws like the Patriot Act to guard the Executive involved in crimes of State. The State imprisons whistle blowers, objectors and human rights activists with blatant ease and impunity.

The lists of State crimes are endless over the centuries and their primitive methods and evil practices have not changed one iota. The Spanish Inquisition likens well with the illegal detention and criminal torture of inmates at Guantanamo Bay. It will always be the

Neon sign of hegemony, rendition and war crimes. How the State can advertise it so well and yet be equally shameless of its evil reputation to the rest of the World, is a matter of the culpable denial of the State in its collective criminal mind.

Why should the narrator now get involved in rubbishing the neo-cons, who are backed by billionaires, without being active in replacing them? If he had enormous resources, what political experience does he have to question their motives?

The other thing is, if the book is factual then why does he make out he really was that American narrator? This is the 'elementary bit of the mystery my dear Watson' and I will leave that to the reader's imagination.

# CONTENTS

References that are numbered (1) to (52) in the text
refer to Google Image sources set in the Appendix.

# CHAPTER 1

## Deception

*They seek him here they seek him there. Those French men seek him everywhere. Is he in heaven or is he in hell that damned illusive Pimpernel.*

My Christian name is James and my surname is Christian. When I began this quest I was on a ship bound for Polynesia longing to paint like Paul Gauguin. In my sojourn I had decided to leave my job and political party and from thenceforth tried to forget them. They had become possessed of a kind of witchcraft, unable to distinguish fact or find reason from their new found powers, gained from political deception.

My party had lost grip on reality. In a strange way they were taken in by their own delusions, preferring the concept of public perception. Even the president was affected and confused as to the nature of things or what kind of facts needed to be presented to the public after the surprise attack on our country.

The nation has been undermined by neo-con elements within the Republican Party who are backed by billionaires; a radical elite that have a global strategic agenda and an obsessive personality. They promote ambitious plans to bully other nations for increased power and corporate financial gain. This state of affairs, helped by spreading false rumours, gives this political elite more power at home by testing the Bill of Rights. This is aided by the use of false flag attacks, the Patriot Act and the war on terror.

Political deception can bring about a change in public belief in order to fulfil certain aims of state policy. The neoconservative philosophy at heart embraces deception as a means to achieve certain goals including state autocracy and an obedient nation. The neo-cons often sponsor the promotion of democracy and expansion of US international affairs by use of military force under the guise of a moral cause.

In the 80's there was a concerted military expansion policy under Reagan. It was after Soviet Russia had become engaged in Afghanistan and seemingly bankrupt that the US should further expand its influence in world affairs, particularly in the Middle

East and Central Asia; having suffered and slowly recovered from serious losses in Vietnam thanks to a policy of deception.

A once notorious member of our party is now a colourful statesman - a kind of Dr Strangelove with neoconservative beliefs; but he also preached 'realism' whilst 59,000 US troops went to their deaths, for the soldiers were our heroes. Unknown to the world, Laos a neutral country was bombed continuously for a period of four years. Not that his realism would stop the war, for political warmongers are bereft of self - critical memory having no moral compass.

The neoconservative influence on the Republican Party, of which I was a member, began to take effect in the 1980's in the US that coincided with a return to power of a strong and rejuvenated Conservative Party in England. But in the new millennium it was the philosophy of New Labour leaders not conservatism that in the circumstances supported our kind of deception. In effect it complemented and cemented our strong Western alliance.

In the late 90's the neo-cons took on imperial ideals with planned objectives set firstly on Iraq and secondly on seven or more non-strategic and erstwhile non-conformist countries that were an imagined threat to our western democracy, before deciding to invade Afghanistan. Immediately after 9/11 our NATO Commander was shocked when he was told about the aims of the Project for the New American Century to promote American global leadership that had been formulated in 1997 by the neoconservatives.

We were to invade Afghanistan, Iraq and Libya and threaten Iran and Syria both whom Israel feared. The others were ostensibly Lebanon, Somalia, Yemen and Sudan. Indeed many of our more influential party members are neoconservatives and committed to supporting Zionism and push the boundaries for war with Iran. The battle cry for Afghanistan was to be the 9/11 cause for everlasting freedom.

## Al Qaeda

After the mid 90's the spreading of the word 'al Qaeda' caused much alarm and prejudice against Islamic sects, justified or not, and that al Qaeda are basically Jihadists or rigid Muslim fundamentalists, fanatical and violently active throughout the Eastern world. The legacy of invading Iraq by the West has unfortunately resulted in the terror fanatics of Isis. It includes Sunni factions fighting against the Government Militia and ranging across the Levant.

The Mujahidin Shura Council was founded in 2006 as a link-up between Iraq and Afghanistan and now Isis, the Islamic State of Iraq and Syria as it sweeps across the Levant and into Libya and Africa. The US is trying to redress its losses in Iraq and demands the continued support of its allies to reinforce stability in Iraq - now a country divided into factions and in abject fear from the fanatical brigades of Isis. And now in 2015 Jordan has had to step into the breech, to fight Isis. The US is even moderating its attitude towards Iran for their support, despite the obsessive rhetoric of Benjamin Netanyahu's Likud regime in Israel.

To hold power we needed to propagate a war on terror against al Qaeda. It was a flawed doctrine of wanton imperialistic design that succeeded in widely flaunting the UN charter and International Law by using false premises, to invade and exploit other countries under the guise of fighting terrorism and bringing them democracy and freedom. We were suffering from a myopic form of narcissism under a colourful banner called Enduring Freedom.

The term al Qaeda came into common usage in the 90's in the western media and is used as a false strategy. Its literal meaning is 'the base' but covertly it implies a data base of Jihadist militants, Wahhabi fighters, multinationals, stateless armies, extremists, warlords, mercenaries, rebels, freedom fighters and so on. It is alleged to be a global militant Islamist organization founded by Osama bin Laden (1) and several other militants in 1988.

Its present 'leader' is the Egyptian Ayman al-Zawahiri a past asset of the CIA who was bin Laden's mentor. A former CIA officer Marc Sageman, a forensic psychiatrist and a counter-terrorism consultant said that al Qaeda is a name for a movement that the West has created. The legend of al Qaeda is now set within our minds, but it is without substance.

According to Professor Michel Chossudovsky in his 2012 lecture in Kuala Lumpur, as quoted online by Global Research: "Both the 9/11 Commission Report as well as the Western media have largely upheld the 'outside enemy' mythology, heralding Al Qaeda as the mastermind organization behind the 9/11 attacks."

The Mujahidin was the principal alliance fighting against the Soviet Union in the 80's, in conjunction with Saudi/Wahhabi mercenary forces and also backed by Pakistan and Iran. Mercenary training camps were based in Saudi Arabia and Qatar, backed by the CIA. It included Osama bin Laden at one time our main asset against the Soviet Union. His code name was Tim Osman. Google: [Uncategorized | 9/11 - Look Again | Page 16].

In the 90's in Asia, US policy required American troops to be engaged in the satellite countries surrounding Russia and in supporting the Northern Alliance - mainly Tajiks, Uzbeks and Hazaras, led by Ahmad Shah Massoud and others against the Taliban in Afghanistan. The Taliban is mainly Pashtun controlled and an ancient warrior race.

## Afghan Resources

US corporations amongst others would provide the infra- structure and sub-contractors for the construction of pipelines for oil and the vast reserves of natural gas and the privatisation of other precious resources in Afghanistan. There are large reserves of lithium and a vast potential for geo-thermal and hydro-electric power. A pipe line from the east Caspian was planned to route through Afghanistan and Pakistan.

According to Michel Chossudovsky: Geological surveys conducted by the Soviet Union in the 1970s confirmed the existence of vast reserves of copper and high grade ores of chromium, lithium, iron and uranium, lead and zinc, tantalum, gold and silver. There is also beryl, barite, fluorspar, bauxite and emeralds. In a 2002 report, the Kremlin confirmed that, Afghanistan has rich reserves of copper at the Aynak deposit, iron ore in Khojagek and uranium, poly-metallic ore, oil and gas. [Afghanistan, Mining Annual Review, The Mining Journal, June, 1984].

The real value is of these ores is well above the trillion dollar estimate of the Pentagon-USCG and the US Agency for International Development study. The Pentagon one trillion dollar figure is more a trumped up number rather than an estimate: 'We took a look at what we knew to be there, and asked what it would be worth now in terms of today's dollars. The trillion dollar figure seemed to be newsworthy.' [The Sunday Times, London, June 15 2010].

## Quest for Oil

The main goal was the Caspian Basin in Turkmenistan and Kazakhstan where amongst other competitors an Argentinian company - Bridas - had contracted to develop the infrastructure for oil and gas reserves of some potential trillions of dollars. This company was in a multi-billion dollar law suit fighting a NY law firm on behalf of Unocal in the Texas courts for several years, over this contract.

Michel Chossudovsky has inside knowledge that 'in February 1996, Bridas Energy Corporation of Argentina and the Taliban provisional government signed a preliminary agreement. Washington responded through its embassy in Islamabad, urging Pakistan's Prime Minister Benazir Bhutto to drop Bridas and grant exclusive rights to Unocal.'

The Clinton administration had given aid via Pakistan to the Taliban in the overthrow of Kabul in September 1996. Unocal would aid Afghan warlords if they formed a council to oversee the project. Bridas sued Unocal for fifteen billion dollars, charging it with under-hand practices in surreptitiously contacting the Turkmen government about their own oil and gas pipeline plan. The Turkmen government stopped exporting oil from Bridas' Keimir field on the Caspian Sea forcing Bridas to renegotiate terms. In August 1997, 60% of Bridas shares were sold to Amoco because Bridas was going broke, having lost the contract to Unocal.

Amoco merged with BP in 1998, which was expedited by Chase Manhattan and Morgan Stanley. Zbigniew Brzezinski (2), a previous National Security adviser was a consultant to Amoco. Arthur Andersen, indicted in the Enron scandal, headed the merger. BP-Amoco was the chief competitor in the Baku-Ceyhan pipeline project from the Caspian through to Georgia and Turkey.

Bridas was formed by Amoco into Pan American Energy Corporation and continued to deal with the Taliban with the support of the Clinton administration. The merger of American and British interests in oil, banking and the military-industrial complex was important to Britain's new Labour government and likely a factor in Britain supporting the US invasion of Afghanistan.

The talks between Taliban and Unocal officials in 1998 had chilled. The East African US Embassy bombings then occurred, allegedly by Osama bin Laden's al Qaeda followed by the launching of cruise missiles against Afghanistan. The Taliban severed talks with Unocal in August 1998 because of the actions against Afghanistan and Sudan, ordered by President Clinton.

In October 1998 a court in Sugar Land, Texas dismissed the fifteen billion dollar lawsuit of Bridas against Unocal for preventing them from developing gas fields in Turkmenistan. Henry Kissinger was advising the Unocal Corporation. The court ruling was against the parent company, BP-Amoco, which had acquired the controlling stake in Bridas the year before. Ironically Unocal and BP-Amoco are now associates in the Caspian Sea basin. BP had opened its first office in Baku in 1992. The Azerbaijan International Operating Company, operated by BP, started oil production on Jan 2014 from the West Chirag platform in the Azerbaijan sector of the Caspian Sea, sanctioned in 2010.

## Lure of the Drug Trade

The farming of poppies to produce opium was more than quadrupled in Afghanistan under the Alliance to help farmers and protect their livelihood. The crop is vital to 25% of the economy producing over 85 % of the world's supply of heroin. The Taliban engaged the western allies in permanent guerrilla warfare where our troops were losing limbs from planted mines and munitions. And few Taliban were killed relative to civilian deaths.

The drug trade was a source of income for the Taliban but there is no evidence that bin Laden was involved. Heroin trafficking has been a source of income in particular for al Qaeda factions in Tajikistan, Uzbekistan, Azerbaijan and Chechnya. The U.S. support for these factions has multiplied the flow of heroin to Western Europe and the United States. [Professor Peter Dale Scott: Global Research, July

29, 2005].[See also Peter Dale Scott, "Kyrgyzstan, the U.S. and the Global Drug Problem: Deep Forces and the Syndrome of Coups, Drugs, and Terror," The Asia-Pacific Journal, 28-3-10, July 12, 2010].

## Exposure

In Afghanistan certain commanders had allowed attacks on villages that were no longer exposed by the press, as for example the My Lai Massacre was in Vietnam in 1968. Except in Iraq there was exposure through WikiLeaks that was very damaging to our cause e.g. Collateral Murder, Baghdad 12th July 2007.

For this exposure and other revelations in 2010, Bradley Manning was held in isolation and without trial for over three years and finally sentenced to thirty-five years. This punishment was to deter further whistle blowers. It was inhuman to hold him without trial for so long under the Patriot Act and the sentence - a villainous retributive measure. He is now a US patriot in the eyes of many because of exposing the serious acts committed in Iraq and Afghanistan. President Obama may soon be in a position to set Manning free.

The case of the moral right for the State to imprison Manning clearly violates the Bill of Rights. However the State itself is guilty of the highest crimes. The US

Government has no morality left if it loses its founding principles. The crimes of the State far outweigh the crimes of its citizens but the State somehow contrives otherwise.

As Professor John McMurtry (FRSC) of Canada puts it: 'The supreme moral goal and strategy governing US covert-state performance are similar in moral principle. The NSA confers the highest honours awarded in recognition of distinguished valour and excellence. These actions are conceived as the highest duty, however life-system destructive they are.'

In the war on terror the press have relayed indiscriminate use of drones that accidently kill non-combatants. The operators are immune and dutiful with a warped sense of power, in the degree of psychopathic killing, some with guilt and moral fatigue. Many soldiers have become victims, returning to their families psychologically damaged.

## Clandestine Operations

In precedence and in parallel a continuous series of False Flag and Black Operations by CIA backed covert operators known as 'Stay Behinds' had long begun under Operation Gladio - Roman Short Sword. This was to help stop the spread of communism in

Europe, since 1947 when the CIA replaced the OSS. It was finally stopped or limited by the formation of the European Union and after exposures by the Italian Government after too many outrages and wanton killing of innocents e.g. 86 deaths in the Bologna Central Train Station massacre. Gladio agent Vincenzo Vinciguerra stated, in sworn testimony under the Strategy of Tension in Italy against Soviet fifth columnists and the spread of communism:

'You had to attack civilians, the people, women, children, innocent people, unknown people far removed from any political game. The reason was quite simple: to force the public to turn to the state to ask for greater security.'

The CIA backed it together with NATO Secret Intelligence agencies providing the training. It continues now in some African countries and the satellite countries of Russia such as the Balkans, Chechnya and the Caucasus under Gladio B. This is an FBI codename adopted in 1997 for ongoing relations between US intelligence, the Pentagon, and al Qaeda. The name refers to the original Operation Gladio, in which US intelligence had relations with anti-communist groups in Europe and against the Red Brigades in Italy, as described above.

Sibel Edmonds ex FBI translator said Gladio B flagged regular meetings between senior US intelligence and a leader of al Qaeda - Ayman al Zawahiri at the U.S. embassy in Baku, Azerbaijan between 1997 and 2001. Zawahiri and other Mujahidin were being transported by NATO aircraft to Central Asia and the Balkans to participate in Pentagon backed destabilisation operations. Thus Zawahiri a 'current leader of al Qaeda' was reporting to US Intelligence as a Mujahidin warrior and warlord.

In 1997, NATO asked Egyptian President Mubarak to release from prison Islamist militants affiliated to Ayman al Zawahiri. They were flown by U.S. intelligence orders to Turkey for training and use in operations by the Pentagon. Edmonds reported an al Qaeda leader had been training some of the terrorists at a base in Turkey. These and related allegations were seemingly confirmed by Sunday Times journalists in 2008 from Pentagon and MI6 sources.

However, the journalists were silenced due to pressure from the U.S. State Department. Edmonds says the objective of Gladio B is projecting U.S. power in the former Soviet sphere of influence to access previously untapped strategic energy and mineral reserves for U.S. and European companies; pushing back Russian and Chinese power; and expanding the scope of lucrative criminal activities, particularly illegal arms and drug trafficking.

An earlier example of subterfuge is Guatemala. It had been ruled since 1930 by the dictator General Jorge Ubico, supported by the US government. His rule was a cruel and exploitive military junta. In return for US support he gave hundreds of thousands of hectares of highly fertile land to the American United Fruit Company, as well as allowing the US military to establish bases in Guatemala. Then a ten-year revolution brought in a democratic Government that took back the land for the people, which affected company interests.

Then in 1954 Guatemala was attacked by CIA backed mercenaries but they were defeated by the people and the terrain. Guatemala's 6000 strong army was not needed. However an insidious radio propaganda and dirty tricks campaign by the CIA eventually caused the socialist and democratic President to resign. It was a covert operation that deposed the democratically elected President Jacobo Árbenz and ended the Guatemalan Revolution.

These kinds of political subversions in foreign countries were extended and intensified by the neo-cons within our party as they became the influential hidden power in the new millennium leading to an ambitious secret project. They conceived a daring and atrocious plan to deceive the public into believing in a war of terror against our own country, by the State attacking itself.

It was supported by elements within the national media in order to invade Afghanistan and Iraq based on the previous idea of Operation Northwoods. This plan in 1962 was for the United States to attack itself and blame it on Cuba. It was drafted by the Joint Chiefs of Staff, signed by Chairman Lyman Lemnitzer and sent to the Secretary of Defence - Robert Strange McNamara.

Operation Northwoods was authorized by the Joint Chiefs of Staff, but then vetoed by President Kennedy. They would put the blame on Castro, thus giving them a reason to launch a war on Cuba. Here is an abstract drawn from an official document released on 18 November 1997, by the John F. Kennedy Assassination Records Review Board:

Use legitimate provocation for U.S. military intervention in Cuba. A cover and deception plan could be used to provoke Cuban reactions by creating incidents in and around Guantanamo to fake hostile Cuban forces. We could blow up ammunition inside the base, start fires and burn aircraft on air base and sabotage a ship in harbour; large fires - naphthalene. Then conduct funerals for mock victims and commence large scale military operations.

We could blow up a U.S. ship in Guantanamo Bay in the vicinity of Havana faking a Cuban attack from the air or sea. We could follow up with an air and sea rescue operation covered by U.S. fighters to evacuate remaining members of the non-existent crew. Casualty lists in U.S. newspapers would cause a helpful wave of national indignation.

We could develop a Communist Cuban terror campaign in the Miami area, in other Florida cities and even in Washington. The terror campaign could be pointed at refugees seeking haven in the United States. We could sink a boatload of Cubans en route to Florida. We could foster attempts on lives of Cuban refugees in the United States even to the extent of wounding in instances to be widely publicized.

We could explode a few plastic bombs in carefully chosen spots and arrest Cuban agents with the release of prepared documents substantiating Cuban involvement, projecting the idea of an irresponsible government. A 'Cuban-based, Castro-supported' filibuster could be simulated against neighbouring Caribbean nations.

We <u>could</u> create an incident which will demonstrate that a Cuban aircraft has attacked and shot down a chartered civil airliner en route from the United States to Jamaica, Guatemala, Panama or Venezuela, over Cuba. The passengers could be a group of college students off on a holiday or any grouping of persons with a common interest to support chartering a non-scheduled flight.

An F-86 properly painted would convince air passengers that they saw a Cuban MIG. A duplicate would replace the civil aircraft with selected passengers, all under aliases. The registered aircraft would be converted to a drone. When over Cuba the drone would begin transmitting a mayday message stating he was under attack by Cuban MIG aircraft. The transmission would be interrupted by destruction of the aircraft triggered by a radio signal.

## Big Wedding

In a similar paradigm built on a fake theme another project in 2001 called Big Wedding would involve the illusionary crashing of Boeing planes using numerous professional and amateur video images, like the Naudet brothers, Fairbanks and Hezarkhani films. These would be released by the major media networks; and the use of two military UAV's in flight to self- destruct, short of precision, one at the Pentagon and one over Shanksville.

It would include a fake attack on the Pentagon using pre-planted explosives but no serious casualties or deaths would occur. The whole event in reality would amount to a mock attack on the Pentagon and the demolition of some loss making real estate in New York.

We would fake everything using scores of actors, shills and false reporting by the media using composite video fakery for Boeing aircrafts; and splicing and image cropping for trapped people jumping from a tower. There would be no deaths recorded by the Social Security Administration; either in New York or in New Jersey and Washington but this would not be noticed by the public. Most of the public would not even notice the media's lack of coverage of hundreds of people in hospitals and funeral services in these cities, since it would be said the bodies and parts had disintegrated.

We would build a wall within a day for plaques and photographs, and later build memorials in NY, Washington and Shanksville. Later, over 700 fake tiny slithers of bone fragments would be found on the roof of the NY Deutsche Bank. These would be offered as evidence of dead victims. In the outcome however the thirty nine storey bank would be heavily damaged and take five years of deconstruction after further episodes of chaos and calamity. The bank would also be accused of insider trading related to 9/11.

## Collateral Damage

The absence of dead victims would go unnoticed and in our defence all legal challenges would at best lead to no proof or just collateral damage. This would be a combined military and media exercise. It would be carried out in the interest of national security, along with multiple other drills carried out on the same day, to help aid safety and add some confusion.

The towers including WTC 7 would be brought down in a controlled manner ensuring the normal safety procedures for demolition. We would use high explosive charges which would also destroy the core of WTC 6. This would occur at the same time the South Tower was hit. Buildings WTC 3, 4 and 5 would also be destroyed during the demolition of the towers. All buildings would be evacuated well beforehand.

Saint Nicholas Greek church (1916) would be damaged unfortunately. Some of their valuable saintly relics would disappear however, including the bones of St. Nicholas a gift from the Czar Nicholas II. The evacuated twenty story Marriott Hotel (WTC 3) nestled beneath the South Tower would be destroyed in two phases as the towers fell, using explosive charges.

In addition the Winter Garden cost $50 million to repair and the Deutsche bank was heavily damaged and deconstructed. Also heavily damaged was the Manhattan Community College - Fiterman Hall that was rebuilt in 2012, at a cost of $325 million. Another one damaged was the Verizon Building (1926), restored at a cost of $1.4 Billion. The Insurance companies, after fighting in the courts, lost their cases and contributed to paying out on all the claims on these buildings.

The FEMA report on damaged peripheral buildings concluded that 56 buildings were damaged in total. There were five that were totally collapsed (WTC 1, 2, 3, 7 and St. Nicholas Church). There were eleven with major damage, three with partial collapse (WTC 4, 5 and 6) and thirty seven buildings with minor damage.

In essence and in order to raise public concern to maximum effect by the media machine, we needed to fake a large number of apparent deaths. Finally, in order to declare a state of war, carry out a simulated attack on the Pentagon as planned in previous exercise scenarios. It would require a remote controlled jet and another drone for Shanksville.

## Streamlining

Then as a result, effectively streamline the US Military, DIA, Secret Service, DOD, CIA, FBI, NSA, Naval Intelligence and many branches of Government by replacing top men with our chosen officers. After 9/11 we would create a new Department for Homeland Security with a 100 billion dollar budget absorbing twenty major Government agencies, including Immigration. We would fail to incorporate the CIA and FBI however.

We would try to eliminate all Union rights but it was challenged by the Courts in 2008. The DHS would be given Seniority and Emergency Powers under the pretext of a war on terror. And finally in conjunction with NATO we would undermine the opposition within the UN e.g. Russia, France, Germany and China to invade Afghanistan and Iraq under the suspicion of them being the original source of this criminal act.

In mid-September 2001 we would pressure Congress to agree to the rambling Machiavellian Patriotic Act that no one would ever read (in time), that dishonoured the 1$^{st}$ and 4$^{th}$ amendments of the Bill of Rights and further protected the Executive from litigation. Only the very day before 9/11 the Defence Secretary would announce to the American people that 2.3 trillion dollars had been lost in the military budget so that it might not appear to be so serious a crime in the aftermath.

## Political Strategy

The event of 9/11 would be a hoax - a controlled act of aggression - a false flag affair but without any intended loss of life. Those in power sometimes control the US Supreme Court. In effect it sometimes puts the Executive and Intelligence above US law with the help of the Patriot Act, as a result of 9/11 and arcane national security laws.

Prior to electing the president in the 2000 campaign, privateers would manage to circumvent the outcome of the election in the Florida re-count where fifty eight thousand voters, mainly Afro-Americans were removed from the voting list. It would illegally void Congress by using the five to four votes of nine Judges of the US Supreme Court that overruled the Florida Supreme Court Circuits to ensure the election of a president who was not impartial to a war against Iraq.

But it needed a more permanent assertive political strategy so we conceived a war on terror. This is a story of an event that would change the world and begin the Project for the New American Century.

# CHAPTER 2

## *Neo-con Gambits*

*A gambit in chess is an opening tactic that sacrifices a pawn or a piece to gain a strategic advantage.*

Our most prominent party members are neoconservatives and refer openly to the theoretical ideas in the philosophy of Leo Strauss (1899-1973) but Straus himself was apolitical, if conservative and a disillusioned Zionist. Two neo-con philosophical mentors William Kristol and Robert Kagan wrote the book 'Crisis and Opportunity in America's Foreign and Defense Policy' (2000). It criticized American bureaucracy, civil service, and law. They want changes in the various Arab governments - North Korea also, along with Iran and Iraq, is part of an axis of evil.

These countries would get demands, certain to be rejected, followed by military action. If North Korea does not soon surrender all its nuclear material and close its missile bases, then decisive action might follow. This would begin with an air and naval blockade. Such action would prepare the way for a pre-emptive strike against North Korea's nuclear facilities.

If we are fortunate, China will finish the job for us by forcibly replacing the North Korean government. France also has not been behaving in a fashion appropriate to a subservient ally. While military action is not yet on the authors' agenda, the basic strategy is to play the big bully and forget Détente.

We as Americans must overhaul the institutions of government, the FBI, CIA, armed forces, and the State Department to prepare for a different war against a new kind of enemy. It is in defence of the 2003 invasion of Iraq and of important party policy ideas, including abandoning all Israeli-Palestinian peace deals, to invade Syria; and employ rigid domestic surveillance with biometric identity cards and public vigilance to hinder terrorist immigrants and sympathisers. Terrorism remains the great evil of our time, and the war against this, our people's greatest cause. There is no other way for Americans, its victory or holocaust.

These are the principle elements of the neoconservative cause. It is said by others that this desperate cry is really a Zionist plea - 'no other way' - victory or holocaust - the desperation not of America but of Zionism. However it would seem the neo-cons wish not to be silent considering how the Jews have been persecuted having had no home-land for centuries. And Israel has given the West the greatest gift of all - Jesus Christ. But see how ungrateful Christians have been to Jews in the past millennium.

## Patriotism

In contrast to the neo-con Zionist philosophy and their influence I am both a Christian and a Republican and am opposed to their alien viewpoint. Otherwise I have no bias against any moral belief or religion since there can only be the one same God, unless we are serenely pantheistic or believe in nothing after death. But Zionism is neither Christian nor Republican. It's about serving Israel.

The neoconservative group have had a big impact in the development of American foreign policies, especially relating to the Middle East. The group is tied through posts in government, think-tanks, and business corporations with family ties and turned into a movement by their patriarchs. The group is truly an extended family based largely on loose social networks crafted by their patriarchs. This is akin to the formation of the National Socialist Party or German Worker's Party in 1919 with only seventeen members.

The USA Patriot Act - Uniting and Strengthening America by Providing Appropriate Tools Required to Intercept and Obstruct Terrorism was signed into law on October 26, 2001. The architects were Viet D. Dinh, James Sensenbrenner and Michael Chertoff. Chertoff was the second Secretary of Homeland Security under President Bush. He was also Assistant U.S. Attorney General. His father was a Talmud scholar. He succeeded Tom Ridge as Secretary of Homeland Security in 2005. The law was submitted to Congress by the White House Administration on September 24th, just 13 days after 9/11. Two of the Senators slowing the passage of the bill, Senate Judiciary Committee Chairman and the Senate Majority Leader, were allegedly sent powdered letters of 'weaponised' anthrax delivered to their offices on October 9. Only one senator voted against it. He also voted against the invasion of Iraq.

## Terror Threats

The Campaign Committee of Unite for Peace stated the serious effects of the act on civil rights.

The government can monitor religious and political institutions without suspecting criminality, to aid terror investigations. It may close public immigration hearings, and secretly detain hundreds of people without charges, and would encourage bureaucrats to resist public records requests. It may prosecute librarians or keepers of records if they say that government subpoenaed information relating to terror investigations.

It can monitor federal prison liaisons between attorneys and clients, and deny lawyers to US citizens accused of crimes. It can search and seize documents owned by citizens without probable cause to assist terror investigations. It may jail anyone indefinitely without a trial, including US citizens. Anyone may be jailed without being charged or being able to confront witnesses against them.

The Homeland Security Act was also pushed through Congress soon after 9/11, ostensibly to aid a government that is divided and wanting in defending our great nation from terrorist attack. The 484 page Act was authored for changes in the federal government. It was passed on November 25, 2002. It consolidated more than twenty existing federal agencies into a single Homeland Security Department, including the Federal Emergency

Management Agency, the U.S. Secret Service, the U.S. Customs Service, the U.S. Coast Guard and the Immigration and Naturalization Service.

The supposed aim of this merger was to eliminate emerging terrorist threats by removing data firewalls between government agencies, and uniting the torrent of surveillance data made possible by the Patriot Act. Civil liberties groups have objected strongly to the Homeland Security Act from the start, claiming that it is branded by three disturbing trends: less privacy, more government secrecy and authority and reinforced government shielding of special interests. The president of the Centre for Democracy in Washington, DC, termed it a law of unintended consequences which is a polite way of saying nothing.

The Total Information Awareness Office is the most contentious of the Act's requirements. It was given $200 million to attain a state of awareness. It planned for 300 million computer dossiers, a file for every American, which would serve as data files mined from public and private records, including data on transactions, finances, education, medical history and public records from every branch of government, including the CIA and FBI. Programs included facial recognition and gait recognition technologies.

The Senate had cut funding for the TIA in January 2003, pending a Congressional report. The HSA could authorise vaccinations in cases of National Health Emergencies, with no certain evidence. Further concerns of civil rights are the HSA's broad meaning of domestic terror - these are acts that affect the policy of a government by intimidation or coercion puts the First Amendment at risk and opens political activists to accusations of terrorism. The HSA was determined to conduct massive surveillance on the public. It approved $8 million aid to states tied in to company data banks. Fourth Amendment protection is nulled when data is held by privateers.

It was said the HSA was a direct result of 9/11. It is known that the Hart-Rudman Commission written under Clinton in 1998 was in fact the HSA. It was published in a report called the Road Map for National Security: Imperative for Change. The Energy Task Force would be free to meet and generate any kind of document in total secrecy after the HSA's ratification. The Freedom of Information Act petitions revealed secret maps of Iraqi oil fields, pipelines, refineries and terminals in March, 2001.

The Hart-Rudman report called for the foundation of a new, independent National HSA, which would integrate various US Government agencies, including FEMA, the Coast Guard, the Customs Service, and Border Patrol. An extract from the report in 1999 foretells impending impotence and disaster at the end of the twentieth century:

'Although a global competitor to the United States is unlikely to arise over the next 25 years, emerging powers - either singly or in coalition - will increasingly constrain US options regionally and limit its strategic influence. As a result, we will remain limited in our ability to impose our will, and we will be vulnerable to an increasing range of threats against American forces and citizens overseas as well as at home. American influence will increasingly be both embraced and resented abroad, as U.S. cultural, economic, and political power persists and perhaps spreads.

States, terrorists, and other disaffected groups will acquire weapons of mass destruction and mass disruption, and some will use them. Americans will likely die on American soil, possibly in large numbers. Despite the proliferation of highly sophisticated and remote means of attack, the essence of war will remain the same. There will be casualties, carnage, and death; it will not be like a video game.'

It was to be a new type of video game using the media to project the grand illusion and thereby increase concern and uncertainty. It was stated that more people were killed on 9/11 than any single day in the American Civil War. This was a clever ploy meant for the public to believe hundreds of innocents were exploded and burnt to death. And the 'jumpers' were trapped in a burning tower and forced to commit suicide, as a vivid side show.

## Power Groups

Of the fourteen members of the Hart-Rudman Commission all are in the Council of Foreign Relations which has included almost every CIA director since Allen Dulles, as well as the neoconservatives including Dick Cheney, Donald Rumsfeld, Robert Zoellick, George Tenet and Paul Wolfowitz.

The CFR also included the more sensible moderates, Condoleezza Rice and Colin Powell. Two years earlier, Zoellick was one of the signatories of the HR report that included Donald Rumsfeld, Paul Wolfowitz, Richard Perle, Elliott Abrams, William Kristol and Zalmay Khalilzad.

The neo-cons lead many influential letterhead organizations and think-tanks such as the American Enterprise Institute, Project for the New American

Century, Committee for Peace and Security in the Gulf, Committee for the Liberation of Iraq, and the U.S Committee for a Free Lebanon. These societies support many of their beliefs and help members of the movement draft policy, raise money and media attention, and lobby policymakers to protect their various agendas.

In a document called 'Rebuilding America's Defences: Strategy, Forces and Resources for a New Century' published by PNAC, it imagined that some catastrophic and catalysing event was needed - something like a new Pearl Harbour, to encourage Americans to support a war in the Middle East that would politically reshape the region.

Elliott Abrams was born into a Jewish family in New York in 1948. He jarred with church groups and human rights organizations, including Human Rights, Watch and Amnesty International, over the Reagan administration's foreign policies. They said he covered up acts committed by the military forces of US friendly governments in El Salvador, Honduras, and Guatemala, and the rebel Contras in Nicaragua. In 1982 the El Mozote massacre of civilians by the military in El Salvador began appearing in the media. Abrams told a Senate committee the incident was being distorted by the guerrillas.

During investigation of the Iran-Contra Affair, Lawrence Walsh, the Independent Counsel, prepared multiple felony counts against Abrams but never indicted him. He cooperated with Walsh and entered into a plea agreement and pled guilty to two misdemeanours of withholding information from Congress. He was sentenced to a small fine, probation, and community service.

Other signatures included John Bolton, Richard Armitage, and Bill Kristol. Bolton is a right winger in favour of bombing Iran. He coldly calls for the death of Edward Snowden but this may just be hot air. Snowden was with the NSA and CIA and may still have protected status.

William Kristol is a neoconservative political analyst and commentator. He and John Podhoretz established The Weekly Standard. Rupert Murdoch, Chairman and Managing Director of News Corp., financed the periodical; Kristol was its editor. He is associated with a number of prominent conservative think tanks. In 1997, he co-founded PNAC with Robert Kagan.

Kristol is also one of the three board members of Keep America Safe, a think tank co-founded by Liz Cheney and Debra Burlingame (sister of Charles Burlingame who was forced to let an incompetent pilot fly his Boeing plane into the Pentagon or was taken out by the hijackers, depending on which story you wish to believe), and serves on the board of the Emergency Committee for Israel.

Zalmay Khalilzad is a Muslim born in Afghanistan and was the director of the 'Strategy, Doctrine and Force Structure' at the Rand Corporation from 1993-2000. He once worked with Zbigniew Brezinski in the Carter Administration liaising with the Mujahadin against the Soviets in 1979-89. He wrote 'The United States and a Rising China'. He worked for 'Cambridge Energy Research', which at the time was conducting a risk analysis for Unocal, now part of Chevron, for a proposed 1,400 km, $2-billion, and Trans-Afghanistan gas pipeline project extending from Turkmenistan to Afghanistan and to Pakistan.

The actions of Unocal in undermining Bridas led to a fifteen billion dollar law suit, as noted in Chapter 1. Khalilzad was Ambassador to the UN 2006/7 after Bolton and a signatory of the letter to President Clinton sent on January 26, 1998, which called for removing Saddam Hussein from power using all diplomatic, political and military efforts.

## The Defence of the Pentagon

In the Pentagon attack on 9/11 there was little physical evidence remaining as it was impounded, so independent investigators were left with photographic and circumstantial evidence. The photographic evidence however clearly shows the remains of a jet aircraft possibly a modified A3 Sky Warrior. Barbara Honegger a researcher at the Naval Post Graduate School and author of 'October Surprise' recently produced a large amount of detailed evidence in her research papers for her book in 2014, called 'Behind the Smoke Curtain'. She specified the mock attack on the Pentagon consisted of a series of controlled explosions including the use of shaped charges and a self-destruct in-flight, drone attack as shown in Chapter 12.

No aircraft can approach the Pentagon without a coded device which the military use to prevent destruction from its own roof missile battery system. No organisation could mastermind such a mock attack using sophisticated weapons, without a vast infrastructure and access to state of the art technology. Washington has the most highly sophisticated defence system in the world.

An article on one of the Pentagon defence systems quotes: This highly sophisticated war-game technology allows the control of several drones from a remote location, on varying frequencies and has a range of several hundred miles. This technology can be used on many different types of aircraft, including large passenger jets. According to Dr Kevin Barrett: 'It was apparently used to stage a military attack disguised as a hijacking incident, under cover of military drills happening on 9/11, while the others provided distractions.'

The attack on the Pentagon was staged so no people would be killed but there was a certain degree of risk from collateral damage which is judged acceptable in the case of national interest and security operations.

Rabbi Dov S. Zakheim was a former senior member and number three at the Pentagon in 2001. He served in various Department of Defence posts during the Reagan administration and was ideally suited for the defence of the Pentagon. During the 2000 U.S. Presidential election campaign, Dov served as a foreign policy advisor to George W. Bush as part of a group led by Condoleezza Rice that called itself 'The Vulcans'.

Dov was part of the Project for the New American Century. From 1987-2000 he was CEO of an international a high-technology analytical firm that specialises in guided radio control take off, in-flight, attack and self-destruct electronic systems of drone aircrafts. Another division of this company is one of the nation's leading public safety consulting firms. They specialize in research, analysis, and management studies in fire protection and emergency medical services, prevention and preparedness, and homeland security.

During that same period Dov served as a consultant to the Office of the Secretary of Defence, and sat on a number of major DOD panels, including its Task Force on Defence Reform (1997); the Council on Foreign Relations; the 'International Institute for Strategic Studies' and the United States Naval Institute.

During his term as Comptroller (Finance Director), Dov had to track down the Pentagon's 2.3 trillion dollars' worth of lost transactions. In 2008 he was hired by President Bush as a member of the Commission on Wartime Contracting in Iraq and Afghanistan. He was Vice Chairman of 'Global Panel America' with Sir Malcolm Rifkind, the former UK Foreign Secretary, Minister of Defence and chairman of the

Parliamentary Security and Intelligence Committee, now resigned due to a recent sting operation by the press in the UK.

## The WTC Experimental Bomb

In the terrorist attack on the World Trade Centre in 1993 a single bomb exploded, possibly a new type of thermo-baric bomb called a barometric bomb that was planted by terrorists. They were infiltrated by the Egyptian - Emad Salem working for the FBI (Covert OPS) according to the late Ted Gunderson, an ex-senior FBI man. The attack was allegedly planned by a group of terrorists including Ramzi Yousef and Abdul Rahman Yasin. They received financing from Khaled Sheikh Mohammed; however dubious.

In March 1994, four men were convicted of carrying out the bombing: Mahmud Abouhalima, Ahmed Ajaj, Nidal A. Ayyad and Mohammad Salameh. In November 1997, two more were convicted: Ramzi Yousef the mastermind and Eyad Ismoil the driver of the truck bomb. [Source: 1993 WTC Bombing: You Tube 2011 Ted Gunderson interview with A.J. Hilder detailing FBI Covert Operations].

Two years later a similar but more powerful bomb destroyed the A.P. Murray building in OK City.

## Claims

After the second terrorist attack on the World Trade Centre on 9/11 the claims were enormous. The insurance companies after a long battle in the courts had challenged the claim by Silverstein and company that he should receive double the amount of 3.55 billion dollars. This insurance was taken out only six weeks prior to the 9/11 event. The leasehold had been acquired from the NY Port of Authority. This double claim was based on the idea that two separate acts of terrorism were carried out on the Twin Towers because there were two planes.

Eventually the total sum decided by the courts amounted to 4.57 billion dollars from close on two dozen companies including Allianz, Royal Sun Alliance and Swiss Reinsurance. The shareholders for Allianz objected to the company managers in not carrying out an independent investigation into possible insurance fraud. The company said they accepted the government sponsored investigations (with NIST contractors) and their determinations. The company did fight Silverstein's claim for double pay out - in total 7.1 billion dollars. This was only partially successful for some of the other insurance companies who had also challenged this amount.

## Prejudice

Dr Barrett is a veritable critic of the neoconservatives believing they are strongly influenced by Zionists or even by the Likud party in Israel. They do get support from a number of very powerful billionaires and their lobbying does help our Republicans to get re-elected. Barrett is also critical of the federal courts: 'The latest example, US Federal Judge George B Daniels ordered Iran and others to pay six billion dollars in damages to the victims of 9/11. Daniels' ruling is only one of a long series of US Federal Court outrages in which the innocent are blamed for 9/11.'

On June 26, 2008, Judge George B. Daniels dismissed three 9/11 law suits with prejudice, including a 'no planes crashed at the WTC' lawsuit against National Institute of Standards and Technology contractors. They wanted to interrogate the government's hired assistants under oath subject to perjury penalties.' Dr Morgan Reynold's case, as well as Dr Judy Wood's suit might have revealed too much information:

The judge's decision subsequently denied Reynold's motion for reconsideration. It established in Reynold's belief that: 'There is no real justice system because the powerful will be served, as blatantly demonstrated here. Any faking of evidence by NIST contractors would have been exposed to cross examination. Judge Daniels' decision defended NIST contractors from the questions they could not answer.'

George B. Daniels, District Judge for Southern NY stated: "In separate actions,

1) Three different plaintiffs, who are all represented by the same attorney, commenced individual lawsuits attempting to challenge the investigative findings, of the National Institute of Standards and Technology, as to how and why the World Trade Centre buildings collapsed on 9/11. According to plaintiffs, the evidence demonstrates that the destruction of the World Trade Centre Towers was caused by a United States secret military directed energy weapon.

2) The plaintiffs' attorney argues that the defendants knowingly participated in the fraud of furthering the false claim that two wide-body jetliners hit the WTC on 9/11/01."

Dr Reynolds: 'These cases are broadly related in dealing with the events of 9/11 but they differ in terms of the exact subject matter. Our claim is that a terrorist attack was not responsible for the destruction of the World Trade Centre complex. In general, Reynolds and Wood focus on proof of fraud committed by the defendants. NIST conducted no scientific investigation but instead wrote up 10,000 pages to support the official 9/11 account. We never submitted a statement about a US secret weapon to the court. Our case only disputed the claim by NIST contractors that two Boeing 767s hit the twin towers on 9/11 and not the <u>cause</u> of their destruction.'

Judge Daniels dismissed all three cases with impunity:

'All plaintiffs, as well as the attorney for the plaintiffs here, are hereby warned that filing further successive untenable actions may result in the imposition of monetary or other serious sanctions.'

Although the claim of the use of a DEW weapon appears not to have been used by Dr Judy Wood and Morgan Reynolds in their joint case against the NIST contractors, Wood did write a book claiming the Government used it. It would appear the Judge has used this privileged knowledge in a broad brush over the joint plaintiffs claim, as if implying cause; and that their joint cases are not tenable due to the novel implications of this cause, as it infers the Government used a secret military weapon. Effectively this ploy probably helped to neutralize all three plaintiffs in their petitions.

Others have said that Wood and Reynolds made a nonsense claim, perhaps unwittingly, resulting in damage limitation against the authorities. However, their honest endeavours now help protect NIST from any further litigation. One other group has filed a 'Request for Correction' to the NIST Report.

## Pseudo Intelligence

In the lead up to power by members of the party elite in 1981/82, Paul Wolfowitz was appointed head of the policy planning staff in the State Department. And Richard Perle was assistant secretary for international security in President Reagan's defence department. Perle hired Douglas Feith who had been sacked from his post as a Middle East analyst at the National Security Council. The FBI determined Feith had distributed confidential materials to Israel.

Perle worked on the Defence Policy Board Advisory Committee from 1987 to 2004. He was Chairman of this Board in 2001 under the Bush Administration but eventually resigned in 2003 due to conflict of interests. He was in various think-tanks including the Washington Institute for Near East Policy, the Centre for Security Policy and the Jewish Institute for National Security Affairs and was on the Steering Committee of the Bilderberg Group.

Mr. Feith was born in Philadelphia. His father, Dalck, was a member of the Betar, a Revisionist Zionist youth organization, in Poland, and a Holocaust survivor. Feith became undersecretary for policy at the Pentagon in 2001. In return, he appointed Perle as chairman of the Defence Policy Board. Wolfowitz and Feith helped to promote the war in Iraq after 9/11 and in steering the Office of Special Plans. Feith was marginalised during the first term under Bush for initiating the Office of Strategic Influence.

This office supported the war on terror. Its goal was to influence Government with biased news stories into the foreign media. Feith gave sustained effort leading up to the Iraq war. He supervised the Pentagon Office of Special Plans, a group of policy and intelligence analysts created to equip senior government officials with raw intelligence, un-vetted by established Intelligence. The office was later terminated and censored in Congress and by the media for its analysis; it was downgraded by the CIA following the invasion of Iraq.

General Tommy Franks, who led both the 2001 invasion of Afghanistan and the Iraq War, once said that Feith was nigh on the dumbest guy on the planet. In February 2007, the Pentagon's inspector general issued a report that concluded that Feith's office spread alternative intelligence on the Iraq and al Qaida connection and other beliefs at variance with the findings of established Intelligence, to senior decision-makers.

So where did Feith get this pseudo intelligence from - the DIA, NSA, Israel or from the Iraqi National Congress and other diplomatic and combined sources? The answer is below. This repeated Feith's earlier involvement as a postgraduate, when alternative intelligence assessments exaggerating threats to the United States turned out to be wrong on nearly every point.

The report found that these actions were inappropriate though not illegal. Senator Carl Levin, Chair of the Senate Armed Services Committee, stated that that intelligence relating to the Iraq-al-Qaeda relationship was manipulated by high-ranking officials in the DOD to support the administration's decision to invade Iraq. The inspector general's report is a shocking censure of inappropriate activities in the DOD policy office that helped take this nation to war. At Senator Levin's insistence, on April 6, 2007, the report was declassified and released to the public.

Replying to the censure of a document that linked al Qaeda with Iraq under Saddam Hussein, Feith called the office's report a useful critique of the CIA's intelligence. 'It's healthy to criticize the CIA's intelligence', Feith said. 'What the people in the Pentagon were doing was right. It was good government.' Feith also denied accusations he tried to link Iraq in a structured role with al Qaeda. 'No one in my office ever claimed there was an operational relationship', Feith said. 'There was a relationship.'

Feith said that he felt vindicated by the report of the Pentagon inspector general. He told the Washington Post that his office produced 'a criticism of the consensus of the intelligence community, and in presenting it I was not endorsing its substance'. This nice guy of ours needed his head looking into if not removed, back to Israel.

# CHAPTER 3

## *Iraq*

### *Iraq is the cradle of modern civilisation*

Freya Stark was an English explorer who travelled extensively in Iraq -old Babylon and Mesopotamia and wrote about her adventures living there in Beyond Euphrates and other books including travels in Afghanistan. She was a kind of female Lawrence of Arabia and loved the desert and the Nomad way of life. It was after I had read her book that I began to realise the uniqueness of this region and the ancient majesty of its culture and she inspired me to think not as an American but as a stranger in a land I could never have imagined.

It was a country with an illustrious ancient civilisation and traditional culture and proud history with high standards of modern health care, social, legal and civic infrastructure but controlled by a dictator who had previously cooperated with western leaders and went to war with Iran. Its difficulties were compounded by sectarian infighting between Sunni, Baathists, Shia and Kurds and now the Isis terror, spreading everywhere.

For the reason of re-claiming old Iraq territory, Iraq had attacked Kuwait and destroyed their oil wells in retreat, resulting in the first Gulf War with the West. Saddam remained in office albeit forcing the UN to apply sanctions after the allies retreated. However the neo - cons took a dim view of this and actively supported a campaign to get a Republican president elected to re-invade Iraq.

Mesopotamia and the Euphrates was Babylonia and in effect the Iraq we know today going back to the 8th century BC. The zodiac was a Babylonian invention and eclipses of the sun and moon could be foretold with cuneiform records and is the foundation of ancient Greek mathematics and astronomy. They had predicted the motions of the planets and the heliocentric theory where the Earth rotates around its axis and revolves around the Sun. They had long determined the constant for a circle known as pi.

It was there that day was divided into 24 hours, the hour into 60 minutes and the circle into 360 degrees. And it was there that algebra and geometry was developed. The legendary Hanging Gardens of Babylon and the Tower of Babel are symbols of magnificent luxury and power. Iraq is in effect the cradle of modern civilisation.

## Intentions

In the weeks before the invasion of Iraq, as the US and Britain pushed for a second United Nations resolution accusing Iraq, President Bush met with Tony Blair. 'During a private two-hour meeting in the Oval Office on 31 January 2003, Bush made it clear to the Prime Minister that he was determined to invade Iraq without the second resolution, or even if international arms inspectors failed to find unconventional weapons, stated a confidential memo about the meeting written by David Manning' and reviewed by The New York Times.[By prize winning Investigative Journalist - Don Van Natta Jr. 27 Mar 06].

At their meeting, Mr. Bush and Mr. Blair openly stated their reservations that biological or nuclear weapons would be found in Iraq. Invasion was inevitable according to Mr. Bush. The two leaders discussed a timetable for the war, details of the military campaign and plans for the aftermath of the war. The memo also says the president raised three possible ways of provoking a confrontation, including a most controversial one.

The U.S. was thinking of flying a U2 reconnaissance aircraft with fighter cover over Iraq, painted in U.N. colours, the memo says, attributing the idea allegedly to the President. 'If Saddam fired on them, he would be in breach.' The idea was not entirely new since Gary Powers was shot down over Russia flying a U2. It was floated by someone whispering into General Hugh Shelton's ear at a Staff meeting in the Whitehouse with Berger, Cohen, Albright, Richardson, Firth, Tenet and others. Shelton's hairs bristled as he said something like - 'Sure and I'll make damn sure you'll be the damned pilot'- so of course it wasn't the President's idea.

Mr. Manning's rapport with the Prime Minister was a key factor in driving British foreign policy in the US, in view of the 9/11 attacks and the plan to invade Iraq. On 30 November 2009, Manning gave evidence to The Iraq Inquiry. Between 1995 and 1998, he was British Ambassador to Tel Aviv; from 2001, he was a foreign policy adviser to Tony Blair. During this time he developed a working relationship with his counterpart, then US National Security Advisor Condoleezza Rice. Blair chose him to replace

Christopher Meyer as the British Ambassador to the United States. Manning took up the post in 2003.

On September 11, 2001 at 8:48 a.m. top CIA Officials learn of the first attack on the WTC: On most days, at 8:30 a.m., CIA Director George Tenet holds a meeting in his conference room at CIA headquarters in Langley, VA where fifteen top agency officials contribute the news from their particular area. But on 9/11 Tenet is away, having breakfast with a former Senator. In his place, running the meeting is A.B. Krongard, the CIA's executive director.

After the first attack occurs, the senior duty officer of the CIA's Operations Centre interrupts and announces, 'Excuse me, Mr. Krongard, but I thought you would want to know that a plane just struck the World Trade Centre.' The centre, which is staffed, 24 hours a day by fifteen officers, has three televisions that are usually tuned to CNN, NBC, and Fox. Krongard then adjourns his meeting and returns to his office.

## Mediations

On September 12, 2001: British Intelligence chiefs fly to US; the delegation visits the CIA and advises it to concentrate on Afghanistan, not Iraq. Despite the restrictions on air travel following the previous day's attacks, one private plane is allowed to fly from Britain to the United States. On it are Sir Richard Dearlove, the head of the British foreign secret intelligence service, MI6 and Eliza Manningham-Buller, the deputy chief of Britain's home intelligence service, MI5. They dined for an hour-and-a-half with a group of American intelligence officials at the CIA headquarters in Langley, Va.

In his 2007 book, 'At the Center of the Storm', CIA Director George Tenet admitted, 'I still don't know how they got flight clearance into the country.' In addition to Tenet, the US officials at the dinner include James Pavitt, (Deputy Director CIA Ops) and A.B. Krongard; Cofer Black, director of the CIA's Counterterrorist Centre; Tyler Drumheller; the chief of the CIA's European Division; the chief of the CIA's Near East Division; and Thomas Pickard, the acting director of the FBI.

In the British delegation is David Manning who was already in the US before 9/11. The British offer condolences and their full support. The US spy chiefs say they are already certain that al Qaeda was behind the 9/11 attacks, having recognized names on passenger lists of the hijacked flights. This was due to brilliant detective work.

They also believed the attacks were not yet over according to Tenet. Spy chief Manningham - Buller says, 'I hope we can all agree that we should concentrate on Afghanistan and not be tempted to launch any attacks on Iraq.' Tenet replies: 'Absolutely, we all agree on that. Some might want to link the issues, but none of us wants to go that route.'

Sir Christopher Meyer stated in March 2013 that just after he took up the post of British Ambassador in 1997 that Thomas Pickering - under Secretary of State for Political Affairs, called him and they discussed Iraq. 'Saddam, Pickering said, was again defying the United Nations inspectors. Would I come to his office the following morning to discuss what was to be done? From then on, Iraq was to run like a toxic stream through my time in the United States.'

It seemed after the first Gulf war of 1991 there would have to be a day a reckoning between Saddam and the US. In 1998, regime change - the removal of Saddam - became official US policy.

More recently in the UK at the Iraq Inquiry (2009 - 2011) a senior British military intelligence official said the hyped dossier on Iraq's weapons programme was drawn up 'to make the case for war', refuting insistent claims to the contrary by the Blair government, and specifically by Tony Blair's chief spin doctor - Alastair Campbell.

In recent secret evidence to the Chilcot inquiry, Major General Michael Laurie, a Director in Defence Intelligence said:

'I am writing to comment on the position taken by Alastair Campbell during his evidence to you when he stated that the purpose of the dossier was not to make a case for war. I and those involved in its production saw it as to make a case for war. I had no doubt at that time this was exactly its purpose and these very words were used.'

It was the first time such a senior intelligence officer had challenged the Labour government's rights about the dossier; and of what Mr. Blair and Campbell said on its release months before the invasion of Iraq. Laurie remembered that Air Marshal Sir Joe French, Chief of Defence Intelligence was often inquiring whether they were missing something and was worried. We could find no evidence of planes, missiles or equipment that related to weapons of mass destruction, generally concluding that they must have been dismantled, buried or taken abroad.

Other documents included top secret MI6 reports warning of the damage to British securities and the prospect of terrorist attacks in the UK if it united in the US invasion of Iraq. Another declassified document revealed that Sir Kevin Tebbit, Permanent under Secretary of the Ministry of Defence and formerly head of GCHQ, advised the defence secretary, Geoff Hoon, in January 2003 that the US would feel deceived by their closest ally if Britain did not join in with the invasion.

Although very concerned, MI6 told ministers before the invasion that toppling Saddam Hussein might give more security to oil sources. Laurie's memo also criticised the role of John Scarlett, chairman of the Joint Intelligence Committee, who later became head of MI6 and was given a knighthood.

## Fabrication

The defector who convinced the US State Dept. that Iraq had secret biological weapons said he had lied about his story in order to justify the war. He was an Iraqi Chemical Engineer who was given asylum in Germany in 2000. He lived in Nuremburg and gave false information. Rafid Ahmed Alwan al Janabi, codenamed Curveball by German and American

Intelligence told the Guardian that he fabricated tales of mobile bio-weapons trucks and clandestine factories after fleeing Iraq in 1995. 'I had the chance to fabricate something to topple the regime.'

The admission came eight years after Colin Powell's speech at the UN in which the US secretary of state trusted the story Janabi had told the BND (German Secret Service). Don Rumsfeld's memoirs also admit Iraq had no weapons of mass destruction. The former CIA chief in Europe, Tyler Drumheller said the revelation made him feel better. Why so? Did he believe, at the time, the information was not genuine proof but was under political pressure to provide such a story?

The sanctions against Iraq were a near-total financial and trade embargo imposed by the UN Security Council. They began August 6, 1990, four days after Iraq's invasion of Kuwait, stayed in force until May 2003, after Saddam Hussein had been removed and persisted in part, including reparations to Kuwait, through to the present. The sanctions were to compel Iraq to withdraw from Kuwait, to pay damages, and to reveal and remove any weapons of mass destruction.

## Accusations

In April 2001 a quasi-branch of the CIA was negotiating with Iraqi Envoys in New York under the direction of Dr Richard Fuisz via Susan Lindauer a US Intelligence Asset acting as a liaison officer to Iraq. After her first envoy meeting it seemed Iraq were desperate to get the sanctions lifted and were offering massive trade benefits for the lifting of sanctions plus allowing the FBI free access to Iraq. Fuisz could not accept this deal but insisted she must warn them that the CIA was aware of a terrorist threat against New York and believed it was coming from Iraq.

Fuisz wanted names and if not forthcoming and anything did happen Iraq would be destroyed. She said Fuisz behaved out of character but warned her that it might be dangerous now to go back to New York. He was aware of two possible kinds of attack a) using aircraft or b) possibly a miniature thermal nuclear device. However when Susan did go back to meet with the envoys, with this dire warning, they said that Iraq Intelligence had no evidence of such an evil plot and could not provide any names; except they had heard rumours of a threat coming from within the US itself.

Susan wrote a book called 'Extreme Prejudice' exposing many aspects of the CIA's involvement in Anti-Terror exercises and the CIA connections with drug running from the Beqaa valley in Lebanon via Syrian agents to Europe. There was evidence that the real cause of the Lockerbie disaster involved Syrian agents and drug running that was covered up. Fuisz himself had hard evidence that Libya was not involved in the Lockerbie disaster. And she talked of her own specific role in liaising with Libya and Iraq.

The main point is that elements within the CIA were aware of a possible attack on New York using high-jacked planes in April 2001. In 2005 she was arrested at her home in Washington by the FBI and held in detention in prison for one year under the official Patriot Act. She was not told what the charges were.

In a live interview she also revealed that a colleague had informed her that during the period of ten days, between the 23$^{rd}$ Aug and 3$^{th}$ Sept, the Towers were under constant surveillance every night. After the janitorial vans left they would be watched and followed home. However, later between the hours of 3 and 5 am several unmarked, white vans would also arrive every night.

Author Michael Collins said: '... her indictment was loaded with secret charges and secret evidence. She was subjected to one year in prison on Carswell Air Force Base in Fort Worth, Texas without a trial or hearing, and threatened with indefinite detention and forcible drugging to shut her up. After five years of indictment without a conviction or guilty plea, the Justice Department dismissed all charges five days before President Obama's inauguration.'

Author Dr Kevin Barrett said: 'Susan Lindauer was a CIA asset who was asked to work as a back channel to Iraq and to Libya. She also worked for the DIA. She was under indictment and a gag order thanks to the Patriot Act. She was convicted in 2005 and held for a year. The only evidence at her trial was that she had met with the Iraqi UN ambassador.'

The most important story she told was that on the morning of 9/11 Dr Fuisz her boss at the CIA, saw a video that was sent to the CIA and the President from Israel they believed, showing the first plane hitting the North Tower. This may have been the video of the first plane George saw in the morning of 9/11 prior to entering that classroom in Florida. The second plane did not hit the South Tower until after President Bush was inside the classroom. Lindauer and Fuisz thought this was certain proof of Israel being involved in the plot.' It is more likely however that the video was an early copy of the French Naudet brother's film.

After getting out after a year in prison, Susan wrote her book 'Extreme Prejudice'. Susan is a second cousin of Andrew Card who was Chief of Staff, the man who whispered into the President's ear on 9/11. The point is that in April, Fuisz needed names of real Iraq suspects to pin the blame on, as the threat was believed to be coming from Iraq. However the envoys were saying they thought the threat was coming from within the US as did several other countries such as Germany, Egypt, France and even Israel and the UK. In addition Iraq was asking for the FBI to come over and support the UN to search for WMD's.

## Plan B

This meant the US and Britain could not possibly invade Iraq under such tight UN control at the time. But finally the threat was decided by the White House to be coming from bin Laden after they had questioned Robert Mueller head of the FBI, over the weaponised anthrax sent to Senators who were slowing the Patriot Act Bill.

That France was not exactly co-operating with the Americans throughout this period put her in a compromising situation and neither was Germany who did not support the Iraq invasion plans. Along with Vladimir Putin (Russia), Hu Jintao (China), and Gerhard Schröder (Germany), Chirac emerged as a leading voice against US interests in 2003 during the organization and deployment of the United States led military coalition.

Despite intense US pressure, Chirac threatened to veto a resolution in the UN Security Council authorising military force to rid Iraq of alleged weapons of mass destruction, and rallied other governments to his position. 'Iraq today does not represent an immediate threat that justifies an immediate war', Chirac said on 18 March 2003. Chirac was then the target of the American and British press supporting the decisions of President Bush and Tony Blair.

## Back to Plan A

A brilliant intellectual of the neo-cons was a leading proponent of the Iraq War. In 1998, he joined other foreign policy analysts in sending a letter to President Clinton urging strength against Iraq. They argued that Saddam Hussein posed a threat to the United States and its allies: 'The only acceptable strategy is one that eliminates the possibility that Iraq will be able to use or threaten to use weapons of mass destruction. In the short term, this means taking military action as diplomacy is clearly failing. In the long term, it means removing Saddam Hussein and his regime from power. That now needs to become the aim of American foreign policy.'

After the Bush administration developed its response to 9/11, Kristol said: 'We've just been present at a very unusual moment, the creation of a new American foreign policy.' He rejected comparisons to Vietnam and predicted a two month war, not an eight year war. As the state of Iraq began to degenerate in 2004, it called for an increase in U.S. troops in Iraq. Kristol criticized Secretary of Defence Don Rumsfeld, saying he avoided responsibility for the bad planning made in the Iraq War, including inadequate troop levels. Kristol was an avid supporter of the 2006 Lebanon War, saying that it was a United States war too. In June 2006, at the height of the Lebanon War, he suggested opposing Iranian aggression with a military strike against Iranian nuclear facilities.

In 2010, Kristol and the neo-cons criticized the Obama administration and Joint Chiefs of Staff for a mild front to Iran. It wrote: 'What form of state would be more dangerous, an Iran with nuclear weapons, or that caused by attacking Iran's nuclear weapons program? It's time to have a talk about the choice between these two levels, instead of refusing to choose.'

In the 2010 affair surrounding the disclosure of U.S. diplomatic cables by WikiLeaks, Kristol said we should pursue Julian Assange and his collaborators, ruthlessly. It also said that the United States' military interventions in Muslim countries, including the Gulf War, the Kosovo War, the War in Afghanistan, and the Iraq War, should be classed as liberations.

According to investigative journalist Bob Woodward in his book 'Plan of Attack', George Tenet, Director of the CIA, authorised the intelligence reports about weapons of mass destruction in Iraq. On December 12, 2002, he assured Bush that the evidence that Iraq had WMDs amounted to a 'slam dunk case'. After months of not confirming this, Tenet said it was taken out of context. He said it was about convincing the American people to support invading Iraq. Tenet claims that Richard Perle told him in person that 'Iraq had to pay for the attack' which was later denied. Perhaps no one wanted to admit it was a terrible mistake.

# CHAPTER 4

## Bin Laden

*The hawk in flight is a dark and awesome sight. But the vivid crow is black as sure as the pure dove is white.*

On September 14ᵗʰ 2001 Congresswoman Barbara Lee was given a minute and a half before Congress. She was the only brave soul to vote against the invasion of Afghanistan and gave a moving, impassioned speech on that fateful day. The resolution gave the President authorisation for pre-emptive wars because of 9/11. And 434 souls of Congress voted after only an hour of debate to go along with this illogical mandate - a rush into a futile war.

What kind irrational fear grips the minds of political leaders when the chips are down? Morality is swept away at the slightest whim and it's not as if they would have lost credibility with the people. Barbara is still a respected Congresswoman from 1998 - 2014. It also shows how they were all taken in by the 9/11 hoax, all that is, who were not in the know. However Barbara did receive death threats for her heroism.

According to David Ray Griffin: Bin Laden stated on October 16, 2001: 'I would like to assure the world that I did not plan the recent attacks, which seems to have been planned by people for personal reasons. I have been living in the Islamic emirate of Afghanistan. The current leader does not allow me to exercise such operations. I consider the killing of innocent women, children and other humans as an appreciable act. Islam strictly forbids causing harm to innocent women, children and other people.'

The man shown in one of the later confession videos 'is seen writing with his right hand. Bin Laden is well-known to be left-handed' and the man's features are not even close to the same. 'And there are other reasons to question the validity of the tape. In fact, the FBI's page on bin Laden as a most wanted terrorist does not list him as wanted for 9/11, and when asked why, a FBI spokesman said, because the FBI has no hard evidence connecting bin Laden to 9/11.' (David Ray Griffin, Olive Branch Press, 2007).

The Rev. Griffin: 'Until the spring of 2003, I had not looked at any of the evidence. I knew the US government had fabricated evidence to go to war several times before. Nevertheless I did not take this possibility seriously. I was so confident that they must be wrong.'

## Intelligence

The NSA had been keeping track of bin Laden's communications with his al Qaida operatives according to General Michael Hayden. They were tracking bin Laden's satellite phone in Yemen for years prior to 9/11 but keeping it from the CIA. He told CBS News in 2001 that because bin Laden had begun using standard encryption and ready-made American telecom products they had lost track of him.

The Hayden interview was replayed on CBS less than 48 hours after the attacks. Latest declassified documents show the NSA used 9/11 as a theme to justify their illegal surveillance of Americans. NSA insiders say that most if not all of the current illegal data programs began before 9/11, but the event of 9/11 provided the justification for the extension of those programs.

Thomas Andrews Drake a senior NSA operator has revealed how the Trailblazer program was pedalled by outside contractors that spent several billions into the surveillance of Americans after 9/11. The smaller Thin Thread ten million dollar programs already in place, protected the 4$^{th}$ Amendment, was more than adequate and cost much less. It had the ability to protect and was efficient. It was terminated. Drake and others signed a DOD Inspector General report that was given to the New York Times. Also, for congress to investigate the revelations of the NSA in 2002 but it was blown away by secret directives from the Executive.

Drake was forced to admit to a minor charge of civil disobedience or face charges of the Espionage Act of 1917 after being indicted on ten charges and blacklisted. The race for contractor's profits outdid the NSA. However 9/11 was seen as a gift to the NSA because so much money was generated from the paranoia that they couldn't spend the billions fast enough. The NSA even defied the earlier Bush Executive instructions to use Thin Thread and instead brought in the contractors for Trailblazer.

He says the American Constitution has been conveniently buried and replaced by an all-powerful, liberty eroding National Security state. Drake had become an enemy of the state for trying to protect the Constitution. They want to collect everything and keep it secret with powers to arrest people under the slightest suspicion of national security disobedience or in questioning Government conduct or criminality. The FBI kept surveillance on Drake and others and eventually entered their homes to arrest them; in some cases at gunpoint.

Soon after a federal district court judge had ruled the NSA's collection of telephone data lines unconstitutional, a different district court judge ruled it constitutional. In his deft and flamboyant ruling the U.S. District Court Judge wrote:

'The 9/11 terrorist attacks revealed just how dangerous and interconnected the world is. While Americans depended on technology for the conveniences of modernity, al Qaeda plotted in a seventh-century milieu to use that technology against us. It was bold and succeeded because conventional intelligence gathering could not detect diffuse filaments connecting al Qaeda.'

A parallel threat, mentioned by George Tenet to Scott Pelley of CBS in 2007, was coming from bin Laden in 2001 and not from Iraq after all. The plans relating to the CIA offensive against 'al Qaeda' began well before 9/11. Two years before the attacks, the CIA had agents in Afghanistan plotting to defeat the Taliban and kill bin Laden. But Tenet says neither Clinton nor President Bush would give him the go ahead. In the summer of 2001, Tenet says he was so worried that an attack was impending, he asked for an immediate meeting to brief the National Security Advisor Condoleezza Rice. George was saying to Rice there are 'gonna be multiple spectacular attacks against the US'. He believed the attacks were imminent and mass casualties were likely. He said: 'We need to move to the offensive.'

Pelley says to George that he could have insisted Condoleeza Rice warn the president to take action in Afghanistan before 9/11. George replied:

'Right, because the US government doesn't work that way. The president is not the action officer. You bring it to the national security advisor and people who set the table for the president to decide on policies they're gonna implement.'

Pelley suggested that George was thinking that they still had some time and George said:

'Um, yeah. But I had another thought. I'm gonna run you and all you bastards down. And here we come because the rules are about to change. Here we come; our turn now. Unleashed, authorities, money, direction, leadership; here we come, pal. That's what I thought.'

Very soon Tenet got the authority he had been asking for in Afghanistan. And for the first time, the CIA led an American war. Tenet thought it was the agency's finest hour except for one thing - bin Laden.

Pelley asked if bin Laden was at Tora Bora and George said they thought he was. At least they had managed to capture Khalid Sheikh Mohammed in Pakistan. Khalid was supposedly the man who planned 9/11. When they questioned him Khalid said 'I'll talk to you guys in New York when I see my lawyer.'

## Rendition

Khalid is still languishing in Guantanamo Bay, allegedly. Indeed this saga is so twisted his trial date is now postponed till 2017. At least he has not been burnt as a warlock and could possibly live to be an old asset and addicted to water-boarding. Guantanamo was to be the scene of the Northwoods Operation. And so the illegal retention of humans was finally established in this tiny enclave in Socialist Cuba. President Obama is trying his best to-day to abolish it, against strong Republican opposition, but the number of prisoners is dwindling ever so slowly. It is now around the hundred mark.

Even the persecutors of witches in 17th Century Europe were no more primitive than the modern day witch burners and accusers of the State.

The interrogators get inmates to admit to other 'al Qaeda' operatives who are then captured in various lands of asylum to undergo a process of rendition. Example: In a court affidavit, Suleiman Abu Ghaith the alleged son in law of bin Laden said he fled to Iran after 9/11, where he was arrested in 2002. This was followed by a process of rendition. He claims he was held without charge in different prisons in Iran until January 2013.

Iranian authorities periodically interrogated him, he says, and they also advised him that the U.S. government was aware he was in their custody. On Jan. 11, the Iranians released him and allowed him to enter Turkey, where he would be allowed to return to his native Kuwait. However, within 12 hours the Turkish authorities arrested him.

After about forty five days of interrogation by Turkish authorities in Ankara he was put on a plane and told that he would be flown to Kuwait. Instead of flying to Kuwait his plane landed in Amman where he was handcuffed and hooded by Jordanian police and handed to people that included Americans. Later, this group re-shackled him and replaced his hood with blacked-out goggles, earplugs and noise-proof headphones. Then he was put on a plane, and once airborne he was in the hands of the FBI. Upon landing in New York, he was taken to Manhattan and imprisoned to await trial. Finally in 2014 in Manhattan he was sentenced to life imprisonment for involvement in 9/11.

## The Needle in a Haystack

The party hawks were not going to get the evidence they needed to invade Iraq immediately after 9/11. Instead the White House was favouring the State Dept. view - Condoleezza Rice and Powell. It meant that Mr. Bush and Cheney had decided to hunt for bin Laden, as they had criticised an FBI Director over the weaponised anthrax affair. The Administration stated that Iraq was not the perpetrator of this serious criminal act. The FBI was left being pragmatic in seeking out a scientist at Fort Detrick since it could not be bin Laden or Saddam.

And so the deception was repeated and another dose of public paranoia was rejuvenated. By July 2001 the alternative option was to use bin Laden since he was quite ill and our agents were monitoring him in Dubai. A senior consulate officer had visited him in the American Hospital in July 2001 with follow up visits. An article in the French daily Le Figaro stated that bin Laden underwent surgery in an American Hospital in Dubai in July 2001. During his stay in the hospital, he met with a CIA official. He was not arrested during his two week stay in the hospital, casting doubt on the Administration's resolve to apprehend him.

On 2 November 2001 the Defence Secretary stated 'it would be difficult to find him and extradite him. It's like searching for a needle in a stack of hay.' But a modern magnetic filter machine could do this in hours. Innocent civilians were being killed by B-52 Bombers as means to go after bin Laden. The UN said the campaign against international terrorists may cause the death of several million people from an impending famine.

The CIA met bin Laden while undergoing treatment at an American Hospital in July 2001 in Dubai according to Alexandra Richard. Dubai is one of the seven emirates of the Federation of the United Arab Emirates, North-East of Abu-Dhabi. This city, population 350,000, was the setting of a clandestine meeting between bin Laden and a local CIA agent in July. A partner of the administration of the American Hospital in Dubai claims bin Laden stayed at this hospital between the 4th and 14th of July 2001.

From Quetta in Pakistan, bin Laden was transferred to the hospital on his arrival at Dubai airport. He was with his personal physician and comrade Ayman al-Zawahari and admitted to the American Hospital near the Al-Garhoud Bridge. Bin Laden was admitted to the urology unit run by an American gallstone and urology specialist who did not speak to the press. Asia Week, published in Hong Kong, said bin Laden had a serious kidney infection that is spreading to the liver and that a mobile dialysis machine was shipped to Kandahar in early 2000.

While he was hospitalised, he received visits from family as well as prominent Saudis and Emiratis. During the hospital stay, the local CIA agent, known to many in Dubai, was seen taking the main elevator of the hospital to go to his hospital room. A few days later, the CIA man told friends about having visited him. Authorised sources say that on July 15th the CIA agent was called back to headquarters after bin Laden had been flown back to Quetta.

In late July, Emirates customs agents arrested Franco-Algerian activist Djamel Beghal at the Dubai airport. In early August, French and American authorities were advised of the arrest. Interrogated by local authorities in Abu Dhabi, Beghal stated that he was called to Afghanistan in late 2000 by Abu Zoubeida, a military leader of bin Laden's organization, al Qaeda. Beghal's mission: Bomb the US embassy on Gabriel Avenue, near the Place de la Concorde in Paris. It was likely a covert operation or a false flag alarm however.

According to Arab diplomatic sources as well as French intelligence, specific information was transmitted to the CIA concerning terrorist attacks against US interests around the world, including at home. In August 2001, at the US Embassy in Paris, an emergency meeting was called between the French Foreign Intelligence Service and senior US intelligence officials. The Americans were very worried, and requested certain information from the French about Algerian activists, without telling them why. As to what they feared, US Intelligence failed to respond with any comments.

French Intelligence was fully aware of the passive nature of US Intelligence regarding a possible threat to US interests and their homeland yet they appeared to be more worried about Algerian activists than any threat from Afghanistan. The Algerian president had been on a visit to Washington around this time. Yet bin Laden was allowed to return to Afghanistan.

The CIA and bin Laden began liaising in 1979 when recruiting volunteers for the Afghan resistance against the Red Army. This was the beginning of the creation of al Qaeda.

The FBI discovered military explosives from the US Army, in the embassy bombing sites in Nairobi and Dar es Salaam, given to Afghan Arabs, the volunteer brigades with bin Laden in the Afghan war against the Red Army. These acts are well within the logic and remit of Gladio B Operations.

In the pursuit of its investigations, the FBI discovered financing agreements that the CIA had been developing with its Arab friends for years. The Dubai meeting is then within the logic of 'a certain American policy'. [Le Figaro, 2001].

In July 4-14, 2001 bin Laden received treatment for renal failure from American specialist at an American hospital in Dubai. He was accompanied by Dr Ayman al Zawahiri plus several bodyguards. The doctor would later refuse to answer any questions. [Le Figaro (Paris), 10/31/2001; London Times, 11/1/2001].

During his stay, bin Laden would be visited by several members of his family and Saudi personalities, including Prince Turki al-Faisal, then head of Saudi intelligence. [Guardian, 11/1/2001].

On July 12, bin Laden meets with a US consular agent in the hospital. The agent apparently lives in Dubai as an Arab specialist and a consular agent. The CIA and the Dubai hospital denied the story. [Le Figaro (Paris), 10/31/2001; Radio France International, 11/1/2001].

The story is widely reported in Europe, but there are only two, small wire service stories on it in the US. [United Press International, 11/1/2001; Reuters, 11/1/2001].

The Guardian claims that the story originated from French Intelligence, which is keen to reveal the ambiguous role of the CIA, and to restrain Washington from extending the war to Iraq and elsewhere. During his stay bin Laden is also visited by a second CIA officer. Last year he ordered a mobile dialysis machine to be delivered to his base at Kandahar in Afghanistan. [Guardian, 11/1/2001].

In 2003, reporter Richard Labeviere in his book 'The Corridors of Terror' claims he learned about the meeting from a contact in the Dubai hospital. It was confirmed by a Gulf prince who presented himself as an adviser to the Emir of Bahrain. This prince claimed the meeting was arranged by Prince Turki al-Faisal. The prince said, 'by organizing this meeting Turki wanted to start negotiations between bin Laden and the CIA to end hostilities against American interests'. In return, the CIA and Saudis would let bin Laden to return to Saudi Arabia and live there - it failed. On July 15, the agent allegedly returns to CIA headquarters to report on his meeting with bin Laden. [Radio France International, 11/1/2001].

French counterterrorism expert Antoine Sfeir says the story of this meeting has been verified and it is not unusual. Bin Laden maintained contacts with the CIA up to 1998. These contacts have not ceased since bin Laden settled in Afghanistan. Up to the last moment, CIA agents hoped that bin Laden would return to the fold of the US, as was the case before 1989. [Le Figaro (Paris), 11/1/2001].

A CIA spokesman calls the entire account of bin Laden's stay at Dubai 'sheer fantasy'. [Reuters, 11/14/2003]. They simply used two words in denial.

## Eureka!

According to Dan Rather, CBS (2002), bin Laden was back in hospital, one day before the 9/11 attacks, under the jurisdiction of Pakistan. Pakistan's Military Intelligence (ISI) told CBS that bin Laden had received dialysis treatment in Rawalpindi, in a military hospital at a Pakistani Army headquarters.

Dan Rather, CBS Anchor: As the United States and its allies press the hunt for bin Laden; CBS News had news about where bin Laden was before 9/11.

CBS Barry Petersen: 'Everyone remembers what happened on 9/11. It's a tale as twisted as the hunt for bin Laden. The night before the 9/11 terrorist attacks, bin Laden was in Pakistan. He was getting medical treatment protected by the military.'

Pakistan intelligence sources tell CBS News that bin Laden was taken into this military hospital in Rawalpindi for kidney dialysis treatment. On that night they moved out all the regular staff in the urology department and sent in a team to replace them. Ahmed Rashid, who has written extensively on the Taliban, says the military was often there to help before 9/11.

Petersen: 'The doctors refused our request to see any records. It was President Musharraf who said in public that bin Laden suffers from kidney disease, saying he thinks he may be near death.'

The Secretary of Defence said: 'With respect to the issue of bin Laden's health, I just am—don't have any knowledge.' The US military advisers based in Rawalpindi worked closely with the Pakistani Armed Forces. He was still in hospital in Rawalpindi on 9/11, when the attacks occurred. On September 12, Secretary of State Colin Powell began talks with Pakistan in order to deport bin Laden, without success. The death of bin Laden came from Pakistan three months later.

Bin Laden died from an untreated lung complaint, the Pakistan Observer reported, citing a Taliban leader who attended the funeral. He died in mid-December, in the vicinity of the Tora Bora mountain range. He was laid to rest according to his Wahhabi belief. The friends of bin Laden, his family members and some Taliban attended the funeral.

There are many reports that bin Laden died of his illness in December 2001, near Kandahar. However before he died a message of his true feelings on four occasions would get transmitted to the world. After this our Intelligence disinformation machine would take over producing a number of faked videos of him.

# Black Ops

Benazir Bhutto stated that bin Laden was assassinated by Ahmed Omar Saeed Sheikh to David Frost before her own assassination in Pakistan in 2007, sadly. She was a very striking lady with imperial modesty and immense courage and very attractive. She was likely in error because Sheikh was convicted of killing Daniel Pearl, an investigative journalist for the 'Wall Street Journal', in 2002. In subsequent interviews, Bhutto spoke of bin Laden as if he were still alive.

Sheikh was a double agent working for Western Intelligence. He is a British Muslim born in England. He is probably still alive and is said to be in and out of prison. Intelligence agencies generate myth. All their characters and events are wrapped in multiple layers of disinformation to the public so that everyone gets misinformed.

The plan to invade Iraq would be put on hold by the White House in favour of invading Afghanistan. The FBI was claiming that the Anthrax virus sent to two Senators and certain press offices was weaponised using military grade silica not available to al Qaeda but more likely from Fort Detrick, Md. The news networks would try to implicate Iraq. The White House however tried to force the FBI to detract from reality by rubbishing their messenger. Instead they would prepare to invade Afghanistan by warning the ISI if they didn't get the Taliban to give up bin Laden the invasion would begin under a carpet of missiles and bombs.

The false story of bin Laden's death in the killing house in Pakistan in 2011 by marine commandos is now explained. Dr Paul Craig Roberts ex Assistant Secretary of the Treasury for Reagan and journalist got the Abbottabad story first hand from Pakistan National TV which is also found on the internet. He says, 'Their reporter interviewed a neighbour at Abbottabad; indicating bin Laden's death was a black op exercise.'

The story Bashir gave of the attack is quite different to the story told by the US government. In Bashir's account there was only one helicopter and it crash landed. Then later there was an explosion and he witnessed dead bodies around the helicopter.

Reuters shows the picture of the stealth helicopter (3) that crash landed over the wall of the compound. Its tail got caught in the barbed wire fence on top of the wall. The rotor tail became separated and was kept by the Pakistani authorities. Then another photograph showed a black pile of metallic debris further away from the wall. If the craft had exploded the debris would have been scattered everywhere. However it looks like the craft was being rigged for removal in day light sometime later. From the sunlight on the craft it looks to be an hour or so after dawn.

There are also pictures of the craft being lifted by a crane and it does look as if the craft had been burnt by the crash. The US official story says there were two Black Hawk helicopters flown in but one crash landed due to mechanical failure. Then it was destroyed.

The size of the craft is so small it might just fit two people squatting down. It is barely four feet high, by four feet wide and twelve feet long from nose to tail. This is estimated by comparison to the two men next to it, who appear to be soldiers working to remove the craft. It looks like the craft was a drone because it is so small and there are no manual doors with handles or external fittings. There are tiny windows in the frontal side but these would not allow the pilot full-frontal vision. Another point - it is unlikely the craft would be primed to be destroyed if there were operatives on board.

The US said they had sent in two Black Hawks and that one had crashed and had to be destroyed. The craft at the wall is not the Black Hawk variant

(UH60) they said it was but a small and secret, stealth unmanned aerial vehicle. Just recently the Chinese have produced a prototype drone very similar in design to this stealth craft for the drone market.

Bashir said there were two helicopters that flew over from different directions, but did not land. His account is questionable with regards to the exploded helicopter however. In the photograph we see rigging equipment attached to the craft ready for it to be removed by the military. This work must have occurred later in the morning after securing the compound. Therefore his story about witnessing an exploded helicopter with dead people around might not be true. The authorities kept the rotor and it would appear the craft was burnt or damaged by the crash.

The final decision to launch the raid was decided by President Obama on the basis of policy since he had noted beforehand it was uncertain the man was bin Laden. Obama had campaigned to get the US out of Afghanistan by 2014. Roberts was rated one of America's top journalists and said the neo-cons are 'brown shirts' with the same low intelligence and morals as Hitler's enthusiastic supporters. This description is ironic considering many of them are supporters of Israel but it is true that some of them lean towards a right wing philosophy that strongly supports the more extreme principles of Zionism. In effect a movement in reaction to the persecution of the Jews in Europe and for the re-establishment of Israel.

The BBC interviewed many residents of Abbottabad. They said that bin Laden had never lived there. The person who lived next door to the compound said that the resident shown in the American photo was not bin Laden, but a neighbour whom he knew well. The Pakistanis say the killing of bin Laden is an American hoax.

The Guardian reported the CIA organised a fake vaccination programme in the town where it believed bin Laden was hiding in an elaborate attempt to obtain DNA from the fugitive al Qaida leader's family, a Guardian investigation has found. As part of extensive preparations for the raid that killed bin Laden in May 2011, CIA agents recruited a senior Pakistani doctor to organise the vaccine drive in Abbottabad, even starting the project in a poorer part of town to make it look more authentic, according to Pakistani officials and local residents.

The doctor, Shakil Afridi was arrested and gaoled by the Inter-Services Intelligence agency for liaising with the CIA. Relations between Washington and

Islamabad had deteriorated considerably since this event. The doctor's arrest had exacerbated these tensions. The US was anxious for the doctor's safety, and is thought to have intervened on his behalf.

The vaccinations were planned after the CIA had tracked an al-Qaida courier, known as Abu Ahmad al-Kuwaiti. His real name was Ibrahim Saeed Ahmed - a Pashtun born in Kuwait. In August 2010 agents tracked al Kuwaiti as he drove from Peshawar to a residence in Abbottabad - and monitored the compound and suspected that it housed bin Laden. He was supposedly killed in the compound along with bin Laden.

The agency monitored the compound by satellite and surveillance from a local CIA safe house in Abbottabad, but wanted confirmation that bin Laden was there before mounting a risky operation inside another country. DNA from any of the bin Laden children in the compound could be compared with a sample from his sister, who allegedly died in Boston in 2010, to provide evidence that the family was present.

## Collective Deception

Thus by 'killing' bin Laden the job would be over, providing an exit strategy for the US and its allies.

It further damaged relations between Pakistan and the US. In reality both their country's Intelligence agencies knew bin Laden had long ago deceased in 2001. The CIA led the Operation with several Military Intelligence Agencies that requested tens of millions of dollars extra from Congress to fund it, including the National Security Agency, National Geospatial-Intelligence Agency, Office of the Director of National Intelligence and the U.S. Defence Department.

Most people believe in the official deception that bin Laden was behind 9/11. They never think twice about it even if they are aware of darker forces. They count on my country right or wrong. John La Carre once said of his former boss in MI5: 'Whereas he believed that uncritical love of the Secret Services was synonymous with love of country I came to believe that such love should be vigilantly examined.' As an ex party member I would say rather that we used our Military Intelligence then modified it to suit our own ends.

The sprawling NSA headquarters at Arlington under General Haydon had to increase its security on 9/11. But the search for bin Laden became the cause of sweeping reforms in Intelligence gathering so that every American and the world became suspects that warranted listening in on for any sign of terrorist threats. When asked why we could not counter an attack from bin Laden yet managed to counter the Soviet threat, Haydon replied bin Laden was using our own sophisticated technology against us.

It could not be put better than this, that we sophisticated Americans were foisted on our own petard by collective deception. And the paranoia justified the war deaths and the trillions spent to support corrupt elements and run by a political Intelligence network that engages in deception sustained by propaganda that can no longer decipher reality, if it ever could.

# CHAPTER 5

## Anti-Terror Operations

*Terrorism is not classed as terror if it is carried out by western Governments bombing poor nation states with weapons of mass destruction in order for them to conform to the Globalist agenda. Instead it is classed as a form of liberation from their oppressors.*

Under President Clinton the neo-cons were already preparing the Project for the New American Century whereby the invasion of Iraq was to be the first objective, but Bill did not welcome it. Clinton was a smooth operator and well-liked by the public with his un-abating charisma. He showed the human qualities of Jack Kennedy and they shook hands; with a big headed swagger able to play a cool sax with a hot blues harmonica. As governor of Arkansas he was co-operating with the state and federal investigation into CIA covert operations covering cocaine, drug and gun running between El Salvador and Mena and associated horrific deaths.

In 1987 two young boys were found murdered and their mutilated bodies found on railway track but the Medical Examiner pronounced they were killed by a train. It was a cover up and the man should have been sacked. In connection with this case two men were horrifically murdered in 1988 and 1989 and four others.

A prime lady witness exposing the parties involved was sent to prison. The Attorney led the case to an impasse. Later, the same Prosecutor was hostile to the Sherriff and other investigators who got near to the guilty parties involved in millions, from drug trafficking and money laundering and loans to local business. The infamous Barry Seal in flying the Fat Lady was an adventurer and principal player in carrying out this operation but was gunned down in 1986, allegedly by Columbian hit men, in Baton Rouge. Terry Reed the pilot exposed the drug gun running in his book 'Compromised'.

In another connection - Celerino Castillo was a decorated war hero in Vietnam and an agent of the Drug Enforcement and Administration. He is known for revealing the CIA arms-for-drugs trade (led by Colonel Oliver North) that was used to prop up the 1980s Contra counter-insurgency in Nicaragua and for his book, entitled 'Powder Burns: Cocaine, Contras and the Drug War'.

He was training the death squads and black ops in El Salvador when he discovered that the Contras were smuggling cocaine into the United States. His superiors ignored his reports. He was sent to prison in 2008 after revealing that ATF agents were allegedly involved in drug smuggling into Mexico. The book was too controversial for an American publisher to print at the time.

Mena the press said is a myth, that the CIA ever ran cocaine through Mena airport, or laundered the proceeds through various financial institutions, is questionable. That such activities ever took place at Mena, amongst other locations, should be fiction. There have been over two dozen killings and suicides in connection with Mena.

In April 1995 our President - Bill Clinton possibly suspected that covert agents had infiltrated the gang connected with the OK City bombing, when finally briefed by the CIA. His tears of sadness at the children's graves whilst planting a dogwood tree at the memorial, was profound. He found out late this most outrageous scheme of clandestine Intelligence to curb the burgeoning anti - Government right wing of America's mid-west, was in order to cool fanatical freedom fighters.

There is apparent evidence from local reporters and medics that McVeigh was still breathing after they injected him in the leg. This procedure is contra-indicated for lethal injections into arterial veins that have to be done in the arm. This might suggest the possibility that Timothy McVeigh was not executed. It is certainly odd how he effectively admitted guilt to his attorneys as revenge for Waco and Ruby Ridge. He also allegedly wrote a number of challenging essays condemning the acts of government including all war deaths from Hiroshima to Iraq and was seemingly unconcerned about his fate.

The consequence of OK City 1995 and the 1993 WTC bombing was the reason for Clinton passing the Anti-Terrorism and Effective Death Penalty Act of 1996.

## Comparisons

If one looks at the blast damage, when comparing photographs of the collapsed A P Murrah Building and the collapsed Pentagon Wedge 1 and WTC 6, they are similar in form. A third of the APM building had collapsed, leaving sectioned office fabrics intact, by cleavage from charges placed inside the buildings. It was carried out using a very high explosive charge; only one of the bombs detonated destroying columns, leaving two thirds of the structure intact. Experts say only one bomb exploded, with a high blast wave velocity, possibly a thermo-baric bomb. The second bomb exploded was in the Ryder truck outside the building.

The dynamics of a thermo-baric bomb is it feeds on oxygen e.g. like propane or acetylene does. Another type is called a barometric bomb and releases a high density catalytic Al Silicate/Pb Azide cold cloud particle mixture from inside a separate aqueous ammonium nitrate chamber, which is activated by PETN in the primary stage. It is a two stage device releasing ammonium nitrate into the cloud via a 'petal' spray.

The blast cloud is focused in direction by a V notched cache (as in a fire-extinguisher) in the steel chamber and detonated by electric discharge. A thermo-baric bomb was allegedly used to destroy a barracks building in Beirut in 1983 by a fuel /air explosion, using propane or butane, allegedly. These bombs developed on the principle of gas or fine dust explosions in mines, aluminium dust in industry, and even flour dust in mills.

They possibly used a thermo-baric (or barometric) bomb at APM but the US Government did not condone any covert agent, acting as an infiltrator into the right wing gang, to plant bombs in the building. The largely Government rented building was practically empty in order to place the bombs.

The ATF were present beforehand because witnesses saw their white vans outside as they vacated the building. Two or three more bombs did not detonate and were defused. Two blasts were recorded by the NGS seismographs ten seconds apart, one would be the Ryder truck bomb. The evidence of dead victims is not at all apparent in any photographs and the injured people appear to be covered in bright red blood but un-harmed.

## Detective Work

An independent journalist called Paul Thompson has devoted his time to studying all the press releases regarding 9/11 and the war on terror. His findings when collated give a troubling picture of international collaboration and the intelligence gathering disinformation machine. The Congressional Joint Inquiry into 9/11 however failed to mention any warnings from foreign governments.

The following quotes from both the media and intelligence agencies are quoted without comment or criticism as they just indicate there was a significant amount of information available to US Intelligence before 9/11. This data indicates how much they knew even if some of their sources were unreliable and peppered with pure disinformation. Here is a short review of Thompson's work which also shows how much the inquiry overlooked:

An undercover agent from Morocco successfully penetrated al-Qaeda. He learned that bin Laden was 'very disappointed' that the 1993 bombing had not toppled the World Trade Center, and was planning 'large scale operations in New York in the summer or fall of 2001.' He provided this information to the US in August 2001. [Agence France Presse, 11/22/01, International Herald Tribune, 5/21/02, London Times, 6/12/02].

In late 2000, British investigators and their counterparts in the Cayman Islands began a yearlong probe of three Afghan men who had entered the Cayman Islands illegally. [Fox News, 5/17/02].

In late August 2001, shortly before the attacks, an anonymous letter to a Cayman radio station alleged these same men were al-Qaeda agents organizing a major terrorist act against the US via an airline or airlines. [Miami Herald, 9/20/01].

In late July 2001, Afghanistan's Foreign Minister Wakil Ahmed Muttawakil learned that al Qaeda was planning a huge attack on targets inside America. It would kill thousands, he learned from the rebel leader of Islamic Movement of Uzbekistan. [Reuters, 9/7/02].

Hasni Mubarak, President of Egypt said in early September 2001 Egyptian intelligence warned American officials that al-Qaeda was planning a significant operation against an American target, probably within the US. [New York Times, 6/4/02].

In 1999, British intelligence gave a secret report to the US Embassy that stated al-Qaeda had plans to use commercial aircraft possibly as flying bombs. [Sunday Times, 6/9/02].

In early August 2001, the British gave another warning, telling the US to expect multiple airline hijackings from al Qaeda. This warning was included in Bush's briefing on August 6, 2001. [Sunday Herald, 5/19/02].

In June 2001, German intelligence warned the US, Britain, and Israel that Middle Eastern terrorists were planning to hijack commercial aircraft. [Frankfurter Allgemeine Zeitung, 9/11/01].

In late July 2001, Egyptian intelligence stated from an undercover agent in Afghanistan that twenty al Qaeda members were let into the US and four of them had received flight training on Cessna's. [CBS, 10/9/02].

In mid-2001, Jordan intelligence said a major attack was being planned inside the US, using aircraft. The code name of the operation was Big Wedding - the codename of the 9/11 plot. [International Herald Tribune, 5/21/02].

Russian President Vladimir Putin ordered his intelligence agencies to alert the US in the summer of 2001 that suicide pilots were training for attacks on US targets. [Fox News, 5/17/02].

The head of Russian intelligence also stated, we had clearly warned them on several occasions, but they did not pay any attention. [Agence France-Presse, 9/16/01].

Russian intelligence agents knew of the assets in the attacks, and Moscow warned Washington a couple of weeks before 9/11. [Izvestia, 9/12/02].

There was an Israeli 'art student' spy ring operating in the US for several years before 9/11. The Drug Enforcement Administration report before 9/11 noted that Israeli spies were living in Hollywood, Florida at 4220 Sheridan Street, near Mohamed Atta's residence at 3389 Sheridan Street. [DEA report, 6/01].

Israeli spies were close to at least ten of the nineteen 9/11 hijackers. 'Forward' the Jewish magazine admitted the spy ring existed, in order to track Muslim terrorists operating in the US. [Salon, 5/7/02].

In August 2001 agents from Mossad, the Israeli intelligence agency, came to Washington and warned the FBI that a group of al Qaeda terrorists had entered the US and were planning a major assault. [Telegraph, 9/16/01, Los Angeles Times, 9/20/01].

In October 2002, the story broke in Europe that on August 23, 2001, Mossad had given the CIA a list of nineteen terrorists living in the US, including Nawaf Alhazmi, Khalid Almihdhar, Marwan Alshehhi and Mohamed Atta. [Der Spiegel, 10/1/02, BBC, 10/2/02].

The CIA had been monitoring three of them overseas the year before. Al Hazmi and al Mihdhar were put on a watch list the same day Mossad gave the warning. [AFP, 9/22/01, Observer, 9/30/01].

So many countries warned the US: Afghanistan, Argentina, Britain, Cayman Islands, Egypt, France, Germany, Israel, Italy, Jordan, Morocco and Russia.

The Wall Street Journal reported that Lt. Gen. Mahmud Ahmed, head of the Pakistani Inter-Services Intelligence, ordered $100,000 to be given to Mohamed Atta in the US. [Wall Street Journal, 10/10/01].

For more details of Thompson's work, see 'History Commons' online.

## Rumour Control

Naturally one has to question, even in retrospect, why US Intelligence across the board were unable to co-ordinate this considerable information and issue an Emergency procedure or the very highest State of Alert warning across the nation. Indeed all of the named suspects should have been arrested immediately knowing the plot was already afoot. The alternative might be that they believed it was just so many false alarms amounting to a propaganda exercise by al Qaeda. However, a Hobson's choice alternative is possible, if unthinkable, in conclusion. It might be that all of the Intelligence agencies including

Russia were in on the Big Wedding plot. After all, Jordan had come up with this name in the first place.

The final possibility is that the Intelligence about an Arab or al Qaeda plot was cyclic and was being continuously fed from one or two original sources. Just like 'rumour control' - an affectionate term used in the British Army by soldiers knowing that Headquarters didn't have a clue about what was really happening.

## Preparedness

There was an anti-aircraft battery permanently stationed on top of the White House, but it wasn't used to shoot down 'Flight 77', which allegedly flew low over the White House before hitting the Pentagon. Instead, witnesses have attested it was an E4B Nightwatch Boeing that flew over the White House. It was a smaller military jet that made the attack dive at the Pentagon and was destroyed just before it hit the West wall.

On October 17, 2002, CIA Director Tenet claimed that the warnings were in a geographic context and appeared to point abroad, especially to the Middle East. [Congressional Intelligence Committee, 10/17/02].

On May 16, 2002, National Security Advisor Condoleezza Rice stated to the press: 'I don't think anybody could have predicted that they would take an airplane and slam it into the World Trade Centre and take another one and slam it into the Pentagon, or use it as a missile. Even in retrospect there was nothing to suggest that.' [White House, 5/16/02].

On June 7, 2002, President Bush stated, 'Based on everything I've seen, I do not believe anyone could have prevented the horror of September the 11th.' [Sydney Morning Herald, 6/8/02].

All of these warnings were ignored, or hushed up, because all of them tied in with the Intelligence networks of many friendly and even non-aligned nations and the International media grapevine. It all amounted to an effective world-wide disinformation network between Intelligence agencies. In any case there were plenty of al Qaeda planted dupes to arrest and blame it on.

It seemed also that Naval Intelligence was to become a mock target at the Pentagon as a number, allegedly eleven, naval officers were killed - but they were supposedly in a bomb proofed room. Some had real knowledge but others were not to be injured without this knowledge; and simply used to swell the number of apparent deaths of middle ranking officers. It is more likely however this reinforced wing, Wedge 1 was totally vacant being the planned demolition or strike point. This feint at the Pentagon would also fix the time at 9.37 a.m. on 9/11 as pre-determined time to declare a war on terror leading to the invasion of Iraq and Afghanistan.

# CHAPTER 6

## *War Games and Bio-Terror Drills*

*Proper preparation and planning prevents piss poor performance*

The Honourable Congress lady Miss Cynthia McKinney her dark beautiful eyes flashing fiercely and inspired with magnificent bravery, challenged the Defence Secretary with two difficult questions. He was momentarily stunned having forgotten the second one. The second one was in three parts regarding the Pentagon's IT contracts: 1) who has the contracts? 2) How long have they had them? And 3) how much have the taxpayers paid for them? Only question 3) was forthcoming with any certainty -Twenty Billion Dollars. Also the DOD/ Pentagon lost 2.3 Trillion in 1999 and 1.1 Trillion in 2000 because of these various contractors.

The role of the new gigantic Department of Homeland Security was yet in its infancy on 9/11 and preparing for its future role. The input from NORAD was the overall key to all the Defence exercises on 9/11 and US North Com was formed on April 25th 2002 to exclude Canada's veto on the US to declare war if any country in North America was threatened, more or less exclusively with immediate effect.

In the case of 9/11 both the President and the Secretary of State stated that no one could have imagined flying planes into buildings. We accept their word and innocence that they personally, were unaware of such knowledge within our vast Intelligence organisations and from friendly nations. The irony is that the President was bang on, right; no one did fly any Boeings into a building and there was no need for NORAD to scramble F15 and F16 jets.

The only certain plane that got close to a building was the white or silver un-manned jet. It was instantly crashed and destroyed at the wall of Wedge Two of the non-reinforced section of the Pentagon West Wall at 9.32 a.m. about 150 feet north of the alleged Flight 77 strike point.

## Serendipity

Even in history there are few cases of commercial planes hitting buildings during peace time. In New

York however a B25 Bomber during the War in 1945 did hit and penetrate the Empire State Building having lost its way on a foggy day. All three of the crew were killed and eleven others. It caused a large hole in the masonry between the steel frames and a million dollars in damage caused by the crash and fuel explosion. The people were back to work on the following Monday. Both engines did penetrate the building via the windows and mortar. That is why the designers of the twin towers made sure no engine could do this again.

The designers of the Twin Towers completed in 1973, made sure that any future plane crash would not penetrate the structures, by ensuring a tight 'Mosquito Net Structure' - a web of fourteen inch wide, boxed steel columns with narrow twenty two inch, sealed windows to prevent any effective penetration from the engines of an aircraft. The hardness and strength of aluminium alloy thin sections in aircraft is considerably less than of one quarter inch steel. The effect of Canada geese shows how easy the flying geese can dent the thin skin of plastic/Kevlar composite nose cones and birds have also been found buried into the alloy wings. However the engines are of alloy steel so could penetrate the more open steel structure of the Empire State building.

If you think about progress, consider the Empire State Building. It is still standing and a permanent icon and the flower of New York. Yet the twin towers were built in a steel web for the sealing in of people and without any real aesthetic beauty but designed for more safety. The Japanese architect might have known the financiers preferred shrewd economics, framed into the modern style. They were destroyed because they were boring and ugly and losing money and finally used as a political pawn.

Exercises

There were multiple anti-terror and war game exercises going on that day such as Global Warrior; Northern Vigilance in the North West and Canada co-ordinating with a Russian Exercise; Vigilant Guardian and Tripod (Trial Point of Distribution). In addition or indeed within the scope of these were a certain number of fake plane high jacking drills with at least twenty two blips on the exercise radar screens.

Tripod was based in New York involving FEMA planned for 12/9 the next day and as explained below, the epi-centre of a subsidiary attack or bio plot involving hundreds of service people, all focused at Pier 92. 9/11 was a chosen date that may have been pre-determined to be identical to the national

Emergency Code: Dial 911 for regular annual exercises all going on at once.

On 9/11, NORAD was involved in an ongoing operation, which involved deploying fighter aircraft to north-western America. Air Force General Ralph Edward Eberhart had taken over command of NORAD from General Richard Myers in February 2000. It had planned to conduct several military exercises and a drill was being held by the National Reconnaissance Office, a Department of Defence agency. The operations, exercises and drills were all cancelled following the 9/11 attack. During fifty minutes of the attack Eberhart was unavailable.

Kevin Ryan an Industrial Chemist is an excellent researcher and gives us more background. 'In the middle of the 9/11 attacks, Eberhart decided to drive between Peterson Air Force Base and NORAD's Cheyenne Mountain Operations Centre. He made conflicting statements saying that he stayed for a while at Peterson because he did not want to lose communications. But he did lose communications at the critical time, by leaving at approximately 9:30 a.m. (EST), when two of the hijacked planes were still airborne.'

This was just before the white jet crashed at the Pentagon wall at 9:32 a.m.; and just as Cheney in the

Command bunker under the White House responded, according to Mineta, and whipped his neck around as the plane was approaching ten miles out, closing in at 450 mph towards the Pentagon, and the young man said 'do the orders still stand' and Cheney says 'did I say anything to the contrary'.

Eberhart failed to explain the multiple changes in the account of 9/11 that were given by NORAD. General Richard Myers, acting CJCS that morning, said that Eberhart told him there were several hijack codes in the system. Yet none of the four planes had called the hijack code on 9/11, so how could such codes have been in the system. General Hugh Shelton the outgoing CJCS was on a flight to NATO in Europe (Hungary) but flew back immediately.

The Happy Hooligans Squadron of 119th Fighter Wing, National Guard was alerted and it seems they were scrambled from Langley, Va. The Langley Air Force Base, over one hundred miles south of the Pentagon, is one of two sites that NORAD's Northeast Air Defence Sector can get jets quickly launched from.

The F-15s of the 1st Fighter Wing were not supposed to be involved in this mission. Instead, that task belonged to the North Dakota Air National Guard's 119th Fighter Wing, which has a small detachment at

Langley AFB and keeps two fighter jets there ready to take off when required. [USA Today, 9/16/2001; Air Force Magazine, 2/2002].

Despite not being part of the NORAD alert unit, aircraft from the 1st Fighter Wing were involved in the military response to the 9/11 attacks. Jets were airborne within two hours of the attacks, providing protection for the National Command Authority and the rest of the nation. These F-15s belonged to the 71st FS and were launched from Langley AFB following the attacks, to patrol the skies of the East Coast. [Air Force Association, 10/2/2002].

Lt Colonel Rick Gibney of 119th Wing, based in Fargo, was ordered to pick up Joe Allbaugh the Director of FEMA from Missoula, Montana and fly him to Albany, NY in an F16. He was attending a conference in Big Sky, Montana, on the subject of emergency response. Gibney picked him up and then had to refuel from a tanker over Fargo (ND).

He said he flew over Toronto and noted all planes were grounded and air chatter was silent everywhere and a despatcher told him no need to request actions but to go ahead to NY. In his statement on film Gibney does not mention Flight 93 and his account confirms he could not have shot it down, as others have alleged. Gibney was awarded a medal for valour.

Cheney admitted giving the order to shoot a plane down and Rumsfeld said Fl 93 was shot down. This could possibly mean instead that it was a drone that was destroyed in the vicinity of Indian Lake, as no bodies were found. An engine was found about a mile away from the alleged crash site.

Imagine, a vast network of military intelligence, partly ignorant of reason, under a democracy aided by the deceit of the Intelligence services and of certain elements within the media, could so easily and happily carry out such a stupid and nefarious hoax on the public to justify a war on terror, excepting that no innocent people were killed in these cavalier acts. But then consider all the deaths and terrible wounding from the wars in poverty stricken Iraq and Afghanistan because of this ruse.

Even the 9/11 Commission could not account for the NORAD officers' bare faced lies that contradicted all known logic and even themselves. It simply means effectively that a criminal network was in charge. It's beyond credibility but such is the nature of corporate evil with such powers to affect decent citizens and sink them into culpable decadence. The military exercises or war games planned for 9/11 are given as follows.

## Northern Vigilance

This was a NORAD operation sending fighter aircraft to locations in Alaska and Northern Canada in a pre-planned response to an imagined attack from Russia. The exploit was part mock, part real. It was cancelled when NORAD was told by Northeast Air Defence Sector that the Federal Aviation Administration had issued a high alert warning of hijacked aircraft. The Russian's were carrying out their own predatory long range exercise on the same day by sending bomber planes to Siberia and the Arctic Ocean. All replicated data termed 'injects' were removed from computer dashboards at NORAD headquarters in Colorado. The Russians kindly cancelled their war games at the same time. Source: 'History Commons' online.

## Global Guardian

This is an annual command-level exercise organized by United States Strategic Command in cooperation with Space Command and NORAD. Its primary purpose is to test and validate nuclear command and control and execution procedures. Global Guardian is performed in conjunction with NORAD's Vigilant Guardian and Amalgam Warrior, as well as exercises sponsored by Air Combat Command (Crown Vigilance) and Space Command (Apollo Guardian).

## Vigilant Guardian

The semi-annual NORAD exercise that had been running in conjunction with Global Guardian for several days and which postulated a bomber attack from the former Soviet Union. Vigilant Guardian is a Command Post Exercise (CPX), meaning it is conducted in offices and with computers, but without actual planes in the air. The exercise involves all NORAD command levels. A number of out of range scenarios were being run on 9/11 including an NRO drill that simulated an aircraft hijacking.

The air traffic controllers who dealt with two of the hijacked airliners on 9/11, were recorded describing the events, but the tape was destroyed by a supervisor, the Transportation Department said in a report to the NY Times May 6, 2004. However a recent program in 2014 on Channel 4 in the UK ran a TV film called 'The Lost Tapes' that effectively 'reproduced' the flights of AA Flight 11 and AA Flight 77 including the traffic controller's accounts. Thus history evolves into mythology according to which version of the story tellers you wish to listen to, since all are invariably different.

## Amalgam Warrior

An exercise called Vigilant Warrior did <u>not</u> occur on 9/11. General Richard Meyers had told counter terror chief Dick Clarke of this exercise on 9/11 by video communication. This was quoted in Clarke's book 'Against All Enemies'. Vigilant Warrior was a Persian Gulf exercise in response to Saddam's build-up of troops towards Kuwait in 1994. Meyers was likely referring to Amalgam Warrior - a wide ranging operation including terrorist attacks by aircraft, tracking, surveillance and cruise missile strikes. It is initiated by the Commander in Chief of NORAD twice a year. [Source: 'History Commons' online].

## NRO Drill

Aside from military exercises, a National Reconnaissance Office drill was being conducted on 9/11. In a simulated event, a small aircraft would crash into one of the towers of the agency's headquarters after experiencing a mechanical failure.

The NRO is the branch of the Department of Defence in charge of spy satellites. According to its spokesman

Art Haubold: 'No actual plane was to be involved to simulate the damage from the crash; some stairwells and exits were to be closed off, forcing employees to find other ways to evacuate the building. He further explained, it was just an incredible coincidence that this happened to involve an aircraft crashing into our facility, as soon as the real world events began, we cancelled the exercise. Most of the agency's personnel were sent home after the attacks.'

In London on 7/7/05 another incredible coincidence occurred as Sir Peter Power was carrying out a simulated theoretical exercise of Crisis Management at Visa Consultants based on several tube stations on the same day as a supposed terrorist attack 'killing fifty two' people. He glibly stated that they were able to switch from an imagined to a real time scenario. He was so enthusiastic in reporting it to the press that it seemed as if he was promoting a business plan.

## Operation Tripod

On September 12, 2001, there was due to take place the second part of an exercise to test the plan to distribute antibiotics to the entire city population during a bio-terrorism attack. Richard Sheirer, director of the New York City mayor's Office of Emergency Management, had hired over 1,000 Police Academy cadets and Fire Department trainees to play terrified civilians afflicted with various medical conditions, allergies, and panic attacks.

Various individuals were invited to watch, including Mayor Rudolph Giuliani, the police and fire commissioners, and representatives of the FBI and the Federal Emergency Management Agency. Pier 92 was set up as a model distribution station where the victims of the mock attack who needed to receive antibiotics would be treated.

The Tripod exercise was a follow-up to a previous training exercise in New York, called RED Ex, which took place on May 21, 2001. This was according to the MTI Report 'Saving City Lifelines: Lessons Learned in the 9/11 Terrorist Attacks'. Staff members arrived early to prepare for Operation Tripod.

Mr. Sheirer had planned to carry out the biological-terrorism drill in a huge warehouse on the banks of the Hudson River. Tripod - 'Trial Point of Distribution' - was an exercise to test how quickly Sheirer's staff could administer treatments at the kind of medical centres that would be set up in the city in case of an attack.

When the 9/11 attacks began, Tripod was immediately cancelled as attentions turned to the real on-going emergency. Because Pier 92 had been set up ready for the exercise, OEM staff was able to move there and quickly convert it into a large emergency operations centre when their original command centre, in WTC 7, was evacuated and later destroyed. Thus, within thirty hours of the attacks, OEM had a functional facility able to manage the search and rescue effort, just four miles north-west of the WTC site. The exercise was later rescheduled and took place on May 22, 2002.

Tom Kenney from Denver with the National Urban Search and Rescue Team of FEMA gave an interview on 9/12 with Dan Rather of CBS. He said no one was in danger in the effort but it would take months to clear up the whole area and for the last person to be taken out: 'We're one of the first teams deployed to support the city of New York for this disaster. We arrived on late Monday night, and went into action on Tuesday morning. And not until today did we get time to work the entire site.'

This statement caused many questions regarding early preparation. The official reaction was that Kenney was confused about the dates. FEMA had said it did not have urban search and rescue teams in place in New York City prior to the 9/11 attacks, contrary to other sources. They said Kenney, in the heat of the moment was mistaken about his team's arrival date.

The explanation that Kenney was simply confused about the date is invalid. Some news sources went to great lengths to dismiss Kenney's remarks. FEMA said it had no personnel in place on Sept. 10, 2001. This is because it would imply the agency had prior knowledge of the terrorist attacks. Thus:

'This interview was on the 13th - two days afterwards,' said Devvy Kidd and 'Kenney sounds winded on the audio as if he had been exerting himself. It is more than likely that, having worked virtually nonstop since his arrival in NYC, his days had run together, and his statement simply came out wrong.' [WorldNet Daily 11/27/02]. Note: Devvy Kidd is a genuine seeker of facts and active today in exposing the truth about 9/11 on her website. At that time in 2002 she believed that Kenney arrived on the afternoon of the eleventh and not on the tenth. However FEMA did not have a record of his arrival as he was sub-contracted - in answer to her e/mail inquiry under the FOI act.

This information however was disputed when Rudolph Giuliani testified before the 9/11 Commission and validated FEMA's schedule dates. FEMA <u>was</u> in NYC prior to 9/11 for the Project Tripod terror drill, scheduled for 9-12. But it was omitted from the Commission website. Here is his statement:

'The reason Pier 92 was selected as a command centre was because on the next day, on September 12, Pier 92 was going to have a drill, it had hundreds of people here, from FEMA, from the Federal Government, from the State, from the State Emergency Management Office, and they were getting ready for a drill for a biochemical attack. So that was gonna be the place they were going to have the drill. The equipment was already there, so we were able to establish a command centre there, within three days. And it was from there that the rest of the search and rescue effort was completed.'

FEMA denied being in New York City prior to 9/11 yet an eyewitness in the C-SPAN video states that FEMA were at the towers before their collapse; and an FBI agent indicated to him the buildings were going to come down. The video shows scores of empty dumper trucks arriving in convoy before the towers fell.

It can be immediately seen that the number of coincidental drills, including an airplane striking a building and employees being evacuated on the same day as the real event, shows how indeed there were planned multi-operations well in advance but also with such a large cross section of the services' participation. This was beyond normality, or reality, in order to increase the degree of confusion whilst maintaining control and safety. Also the Mayor was able to coordinate all his staff from Pier 92.

## Liquid Steel

The whole of the subterranean Trade Centre became a self-propagating molten foundry as rivers of molten steel continued to melt in an exothermic runaway for many weeks as recorded from satellite thermal imaging by the USGS and NASA. Yet Mr. Gross of NIST filmed on video, denied there was any evidence of molten metal and asked a journalist to provide him with this evidence from NASA, which he then ignored.

In response to requests from the Environmental Protection Agency, through the US Geological Survey, NASA flew a plane over the site of the WTC complex, equipped with a remote sensing instrument called AVIRIS. It was able to remotely record the near-infrared signature of heat. Analysis of the data it collects indicates temperatures at Ground Zero of above 800 degrees Fahrenheit, with some areas above 1,300 degrees. On September 16, dozens of hot spots were seen, but by September 23, only four or five remained.

These residual temperatures are not a signature of normal controlled demolition methods which do not use exothermic compounds to melt steel in runaway reactions. In effect this was an overkill project using incendiaries with explosives and probably remote control initiators, thereby using radio signals to activate the electronic detonation sequence. This was evident on the South Tower's destruction, as the tower began to topple it was rapidly disintegrated.

AFP report: "The seismic data (4) recorded at Lamont – Doherty Earth Observatory, Columbia University confirms the greatest intensity of shock occurred during the ten second collapse stage, before hitting the ground. And it was nearly the same for both towers. A 'sharp spike of short duration' is how seismologist Thorne Lay of University of California at Santa Cruz told AFP an underground high energy explosion would appear on a seismograph.

The two unexplained spikes are more than twenty times the amplitude of the other seismic waves associated with the collapses and occurred in the East-West seismic recording as the buildings began to fall. Lerner-Lam told AFP that a 10-fold increase in wave amplitude indicates a 100-fold increase in energy released. 'These short-period surface waves reflect the interaction between the ground and the building foundation, according to a report from Columbia Earth Institute.'"

## Foreknowledge

In WTC 7 we have the evidence of Barry Jennings of the Office of Emergency Management. He stated he had 'walked over bodies' in WTC 7 and later modified this saying he only thought he saw bodies. Barry has since died of a heart attack and it is so tragic for his family. He had related his story to 'Loose Change' and then clarified his statement that he did not actually mean he saw any 'dead bodies' to the BBC. It suggests that Barry had initially given the wrong impression to Loose Change by mistake.

This building was 'pulled' as stated by Larry Silverstein the co- leaseholder, when they made the decision to pull because there had been 'such a great loss of life, I guess the smartest thing to do is to pull it' he quoted on video to the press. Later he corrected the statement by saying he meant to say - 'pull the firemen from the building'. His poor English grammar must have been the cause of his mistaken statement. All the firemen had been evacuated earlier in the day.

Ironically if he did know the building was coming down then this would explain, in part, how the BBC managed to report how it had fallen twenty minutes before it did fall at 5.20 p.m. The BBC apologised for this mistake but said Reuters had given them this information and that they were not involved in any conspiracy. The WTC 7 building was clearly standing behind the reporter as she gave the story of how it had fallen.

Mayor Giuliani was using it has his command headquarters and its tenants were Financial and Government agencies including the DoD, IRS, CIA, Secret Service and Security & Exchange Commission. It also housed Insurance and Banks including the NAIC and American Express. Indeed it was the nerve centre of the Office of Emergency Management headed by Mr. Hess on the 23rd floor. This floor had fifteen million dollars' worth of renovations, including independent and secure air and water supplies, and bullet and bomb resistant windows.

It is sure no lives were lost in this building as the Secret Service ensured complete evacuation, including the firemen, well beforehand as we have seen on film. And Senator John Kerry stated that the 47 story WTC 7 building was brought down in a 'controlled fashion' in response to a public question. And it was officially stated that no lives were lost in this building. In addition no lives were lost in buildings 3, 4, 5 and 6 according to the press who stated these buildings were evacuated earlier in the day.

# CHAPTER 7

## The Anthrax Scare

*Allah is Good. Allah is Great.*
*Allah gave them Anthrax to take.*

In addition to the Tripod exercise another bio terror exercise was scheduled to blame al Qaeda or Iraq that included the posting of at least four letters stating Allah is Great, Death to the US and Death to Israel on 18/09 and 25/09. They contained the deadly Military Grade Anthrax - Ames strain spores embedded or coated in either micro-silica or pure nano-silicon. Up to 1.6 % Si was found in the spores well above natural levels.

The recipients allegedly marked for death were two democratic Senators and several media offices, including ABC, NBC, National Enquirer, the Sun and New York Post. It is alleged that five people died and seventeen others became infected.

Immediately after the anthrax attacks, White House officials repeatedly pressured the FBI Director to prove that they were a second-wave assault by al Qaeda following the 9/11 attacks. During the President's morning intelligence briefings, the head of the FBI was heavily criticised for not providing any evidence that the killer spores was the work of the clever mastermind bin Laden.

They really wanted to blame somebody in the Middle East, the retired senior FBI official stated. The FBI knew that the anthrax used was an advanced biological formula and unlikely to have been made outside the US by bin Laden.

The Guardian reported in early October that American scientists had implicated Iraq as the source of the anthrax, and the next day the Wall St. Journal editorialised that al Qaeda perpetrated the mailings, with Iraq the source of the anthrax. A few days later, John McCain suggested on the Late Show with David Letterman that the anthrax may have come from Iraq. The next week ABC News did a series of reports stating that three or four sources had identified bentonite, natural super fine clay, as an ingredient in the anthrax preparations, implicating Iraq.

The White House stated there was no bentonite in the anthrax. Some journalists repeated ABC's bentonite report for several years, even after the invasion of Iraq, as evidence that Saddam not only possessed weapons of mass destruction, but had used them in attacks on the United States.

One source - the FBI was saying there was no possibility of bin Laden doing it. The other source ABC saying it was Iraq. But the White House was trying to implicate bin Laden, as the President stated so only two days after 9/11. This was an exercise of pure disinformation, or plain stupidity, leading to fixing the blame on the country the US was pre-prepared to attack - Afghanistan because Iraq was not yet compromised, being protected by the UN. And Hans Blix, Dr Kelly and other UN inspectors were a key link in this protection having found no evidence of WMD's. The UK also advised Washington against any premature attack on Iraq the day after 9/11. And Colin Powell was opposing the hawks by saying the UN would not condone an invasion of Iraq.

The FBI suspected a scientist called Bruce Edwards Ivins at the Bio - Weapons Establishment at Fort Detrick, Maryland and investigated him until he eventually committed suicide in 2008. The US Army

Medical Research Institute of Infectious Diseases had been the chief consultants to the FBI on scientific aspects of the 2001 Anthrax attacks. The FBI had investigated others including Steven Hatfill. He successfully challenged the Government, suing them for 5.8 million dollars.

In July 2008, a top U.S. biodefence researcher at the US Army Medical Research Institute of Infectious Diseases committed suicide just as the FBI was about to lay charges relating to the incidents. Bruce Ivins, who had worked there for eighteen years, had been told about the impending prosecution. Although the attack anthrax used was of different grades, it was all of the same bacterial strain. The Ames strain was subsequently sent to fifteen bio-research labs within the U.S. and six locations overseas.

## Back Room Boys

According to two Washington Post Staff writers: 'An Army biological and chemical warfare facility in Utah has been researching a virulent, weapons-grade formulation of anthrax spores for years, and samples of the bacteria were transported between Dugway and Fort Detrick over the years, according to shipping records.'

The Ames strain were grown and processed at Dugway eighty miles from Salt Lake City. No other nation is known to have made weapons-grade Ames. The FBI said the attacks were the work of a domestic terrorist, someone with knowledge of microbiology. Dugway has often processed non-virulent bacteria into dry powdery forms that mimic weapons-grade anthrax in experiments.

Army and other officials have said the anthrax spores in the letter to the Senate Majority Leader were highly concentrated into a powder, down to particles three microns in diameter that would make them deadly if released into the air. They were mixed with silica, an additive. Army officials in Washington said that in some cases, when Dugway scientists want to work on dried spores without risk of infection, they ship them to Detrick first, to be sterilized.

A shipment to Fort Detrick left Dugway on June 27, 2001. The spores were to be irradiated at the Maryland laboratory. They stayed at Fort Detrick for over two months before being shipped back to Dugway on Sept. 4, less than a month before the bioterrorist attacks began with an alleged Florida photo editor's fatal case of anthrax.

New revelations about the technical sophistication of the material used in the letters to two Senators had failed to determine the people behind the attacks. Some prominent anthrax experts believe the signs point to the U.S. biological weapons program or one of its contractors. The anthrax in the letters was probably made and weaponized in a U.S. government or contractor laboratory said a leading microbiologist and director of the Federation of American Scientists' Working Group on Biological Weapons. She confirmed this from an analysis released by the federation, as a part of the U.S. biodefence program.

A former Army colonel who directed the U.N. biological weapons inspection team in Iraq, said 'The quality of the product in the letter to the Senators was better than that found in the Soviet, U.S. or Iraqi program, certainly in terms of the purity and concentration of spore particles.'

## Public Presumption

The effect of this exercise was to further spread propaganda to reinforce the need for a war on terror. One of the masters of myth clique is Philip Zelikow, the attorney appointed joint-head of the 9/11 Commission Report with Tom Kean. Philip wrote a book called 'Why People Don't Trust Government.'

One of his areas of expertise is Public Mythology or 'Public Presumption'. While at Harvard he wrote about the disguise of history in policymaking. He noted contemporary history is guided by those critical elements that effect the public's presumptions about what might appear to have happened.

The idea of public presumption is akin to the idea of public myth but without the down-play invoked by the word myth. Such presumptions are beliefs that are not certain but are shared in common within the relevant political community. Zelikow wrote in his 'Catastrophic Terrorism' about his own fears of some such event. Philip to give him credit warned the Bush administration that the abuse of prisoners through enhanced interrogation could constitute war crimes.

He wrote in 1998 as a result of the 1993 WTC bombing: '... the most serious constraint on current policy of nonaggression is lack of imagination. An act of catastrophic terrorism that killed tens of thousands of people or disrupted the necessities of life for hundreds of thousands, or even millions, would be a watershed event in America's history. Constitutional liberties would be challenged as the United States sought to protect itself from further attacks by pressing against allowable limits in surveillance of citizens, detention of suspects, and the use of deadly force. Like Pearl Harbour, such an event would divide our past and future into a before and after. Our leaders will be judged negligent for not addressing catastrophic terrorism more urgently.'

He who had jointly concluded the 9/11 Commission Report, got his doctorate in Public Myths by imagining such an event. On 9/11 some first-hand reports gave us the truth. These were quickly disguised by the media as they retold the myth the way Zelikow feared it might happen.

# CHAPTER 8

## The Big Wedding

*Sander Hicks wrote a book called The Big Wedding implying that this was the secret name of the 9/11 plot known to all the intelligence agencies. But intelligence is not their real business in as much as it is in their forte for the dissemination of intrigue.*

The investigation into the cause and perpetrators of 9/11 known secretly as the Big Wedding was coded Penttbom (Pentagon Twin Towers Bombing) by the FBI even though it was not supposed to be a bombing. The culprits were quickly identified and evidence of the hijackers was made available within several days because many were already on FBI files. It was a curious fluke of nature that a passport belonging to Satam Muhammad al Suqami was recovered. Satam was a Saudi, who applied for and received a two-year tourist/business visa in Riyadh, Saudi Arabia.

The Penttbom Investigation was the largest criminal inquiry in FBI history. It was launched on 9/11 and involved 4,000 special agents and 3,000 professional employees. The FBI was able to identify the nineteen hijackers within a matter of days as few suspects made any effort to conceal their names on flight, credit card, and other records.

## Cloak and Dagger

Many of the Arab hijackers were being monitored by Security agents with detailed knowledge of their assets, having provided them with visas through Jeddah, Riyadh or the United Emirates. The following characters and details are cast into a modern flint and gunpowder plot, cloak and dagger style.

One month after the attacks, the Secretary of Defence told an investigative reporter at Parade Magazine that: 'Here we're talking about plastic knives and using an American Airlines flight filled with our citizens, and the missile to damage this building and similar (inaudible) that damaged the World Trade Center. The only way to deal with this problem is by taking the battle to the terrorists, wherever they are, and dealing with them.' [Parade Reporter Lyric Wallwork Winik -10/12/01]. [From a US Department of Defence News Transcript online].

Three of the hijackers carried copies of an identical handwritten letter, in Arabic that was found in three separate locations. The first was in the suitcase of Mohamed Atta that did not make the connection to American Airlines Flight 11 that crashed into the North Tower. The second was in a vehicle parked at Washington Dulles International Airport that belonged to hijacker Nawaf al Hazmi. The third was found at the crash site of United Airlines Flight 93 in Shanksville.

The FBI took control of the Shanksville site. Any remains of ash, after sampling by the coroner and the ATF, were disposed of in the Dover landfill in Delaware along with the remains from the Pentagon, according to official records. In addition no bodies or body parts were found at first according to the coroner until he was asked to go back and check again. He then stated later that he did manage to find a few body parts such as arms and legs.

According to testimony by Susan Ginsberg, a staff member of the National Commission on Terrorist Attacks on the US, in the January 26, 2004 Public

Hearing: 'Four of the hijackers passports have survived in whole or in part. Two were recovered from the crash site of United Airlines flight 93 in Pennsylvania. These were the passports of Ziad Jarrah and Saeed al Ghamdi. One belonged to a hijacker on American Airlines Flight 11, the passport of Satam al Suqami. A passer-by picked it up in Vesey St., and gave it to a NYPD detective shortly before the towers collapsed.

The fourth passport was recovered from luggage that did not make it from a Portland flight to Boston on to the connecting flight which was Flight 11. This was the passport of Abdul-Aziz Almari [sic] (al Omari). Yet how he got onto planes at both airports is a mystery or just another line.

In addition to these four, some digital copies of the hijacker's passports were recovered in post 9/11 operations. Two of the passports that have survived; those of Satam al Suqami and Abdul-Aziz al Omari, were clearly doctored. These were manipulated in a fraudulent manner in ways that have been associated with al Qaeda.'

The FBI said Suqami first arrived in the U.S. on April 23, 2001, with a visa that allowed him to remain in the country until May 21 and not two years. However, at least five residents of the Spanish Trace

Apartments claim to recognize the photographs of both Suqami and Salem al Hazmi as living in the San Antonio complex earlier than April.

These residents claim to have known the hijackers and that the FBI photographs of Suqami and Hazmi are reversed. However they both look similar to the visa picture because of the head dress in the visa. Other reports conflictingly suggested that Suqami was staying with Waleed al Shehri in Hollywood, Florida.

On May 19, Suqami and Wail al Shehri took a flight from Fort Lauderdale to Freeport, Bahamas where they had reservations at the Princess Resort. Lacking proper documentation they were stopped upon landing, and returned to Florida the same day and rented a red Kia Rio. Suqami opened a bank account with a cash deposit around June 2001, and on July 3 he was issued a Florida State Identification Card. He also used his Saudi license to gain a Florida drivers' license bearing the same home address as Wail al Shehri, at a hotel in Boynton Beach.

Despite this, the 9/11 Commission claims that Suqami was the only hijacker not to have any form of US identification. Suqami, Wail and Waleed al Shehri purchased one month passes to a Boynton Beach gym. Muhammad Atta and Marwan al Shehhi also reportedly trained at a gym, in Delray Beach.

CIA director George Tenet later said that they probably were told little more than that they were headed for a suicide mission inside the United States. Tenet is well known to have brilliant insight and is a swarthy Greek American - a challenging if not an intemperate and intimidating character full of passionate, articulated slang.

On September 10, 2001, Suqami shared a room at a hotel in Boston with three of the UA Flight 175 hijackers, Marwan al Shehhi, Fayez Banihammad and Mohand al Shehri. On the day of the attacks, Suqami checked in at the flight desk using his Saudi passport, and boarded AA Flight 11. At Logan International Airport, he was selected by CAPPS which required his checked bags to undergo extra screening for explosives and involved no extra screening at the passenger security checkpoint. Other sources provide evidence of CCT footage of two of the alleged hijackers going through airport security at Portland, Maine.

On the AA Flight 11 from Boston to LA was David Angell one of the screen writers for the famous TV shows Cheers and Frasier, and his wife Lynn. However they had cancelled their flight two weeks beforehand. Then they re-booked the flight and so both allegedly died on 9/11. The mystery of the phantom Flight 11 deepens when we examine its connections to various film documentaries with tentacles into Hollywood and various associated TV channels e.g. the 'Frasier' connection in a clip seen on U-tube and Channel Four's - 'The Missing Tapes.'

All of the nineteen hijackers (5) listed by the FBI have not been withdrawn even though they admit now that a number of them may still be alive. So they accept a few were mistaken identities. It does not change the account of the Big Wedding plot however. Two of nineteen suspects named by the FBI, Saeed al Ghamdi and Ahmed al Ghamdi, have the same names as men listed at a housing facility for foreign military trainees at Pensacola. Two others, Hamza al Ghamdi and Ahmed al Nami, have names similar to individuals listed in public records as using the same address inside the base.

A man named Saeed al Ghamdi graduated from the Defence Language Institute at Lackland Air Force Base in San Antonio. Two men with the same names as two other hijackers, Mohamed Atta and Abdulaziz al Omari, were graduates of the U.S. International

Officers School at Maxwell Air Force Base, Ala., and the Aerospace Medical School at Brooks Air Force Base in San Antonio, respectively.

We see a number of similar names partly due to the erratic or duplicative nature of clandestine affairs and the mixing up of names, identities and incorrect abbreviations. An FBI notice to banks on Sept.19 raised the possibility that Khalid al Mihdhar might still be alive without speculating or explaining how that could be possible. One of the three al Shehri's in the photographs protested his innocence from Casablanca, Morocco.

A man named by the US Department of Justice is alive and living in Jeddah. Abdul al Omari is a pilot with Saudi Airlines and visited the US consulate in Jeddah to demand an explanation: 'The name listed is my name and the birth date is the same as mine, but I was not the hijacker as you can see', he told the London-based Asharq al Awsat newspaper.

Yet another Abdul Aziz al Omari hijacker of Fl.11 said that he was at his desk at the Saudi telecoms authority in Riyadh when the attacks took place. He is an engineer with Saudi Telecoms, and lost his passport while studying in Denver. The Saudi Airlines pilot, Saeed al Ghamdi, is furious that the hijackers' personal details - including name, place, date of birth and occupation - matched his own. Note the duplicating and even triplicating of names by the FBI detective work in the shots.

Two of them were brothers. Salem al Hazmi is 26 and had just returned to work at a petro-chemical complex in the industrial eastern city of Yanbu after a holiday in Saudi Arabia on 9/11. He was accused of hijacking AA Flight 77 and said 'I have never been to the United States and have not been out of Saudi Arabia in the past two years.' He claimed that his passport had been stolen by a pickpocket in Cairo three years before. Ahmed al Nami, 33, from Riyadh, an administrative supervisor with Saudi Arabian Airlines, said that he was in Riyadh when the terrorists struck. He said: 'I'm still alive, as you can see. I was shocked to see my name mentioned by the American Justice Department'.

Atta's father claimed that his son had called him two days after the attack. A man by the same name is a pilot, whose father is a Saudi diplomat in Bombay. 'I personally talked to both father and son today,' said Gaafar Allagany, head of the Saudi Embassy's information centre. In 1995 another Mohamed Atta spent three months with co-students Volker Hauth and

Ralph Bodenstein in Cairo. Yet another Mohamed Atta trained at the International Officer's School at Maxwell/ Gunter Air Force Base in Montgomery, Alabama.

In 1996 when the term al Qaeda was first mentioned in the US media, four of the hijackers, or people with the same names as the hijackers, were being trained at Pensacola Naval Air Station in the USA. Mohand al Shehri is still alive in Morocco. The CIA suspected Ziad Jarrah had been in Afghanistan and wanted him questioned because of his alleged involvement in terrorist activities, UAE sources said. A CIA spokesman denied that they knew anything about Jarrah before 9/11 or had anything do with his questioning in Dubai. The father of Saeed al Ghamdi told the Al Watan newspaper that the picture provided by the FBI was not that of his son. 'It has no resemblance to him at all,' he said.

At Freeway Airport in Bowie, Md., twenty miles west of Washington, a flight instructor instantly recognized the name of alleged hijacker Hani Hanjour when the FBI released a list of nineteen suspects in the four hijackings. Hanjour, the only suspect on Flight 77 the FBI listed as a pilot, had come to the airport one month earlier seeking to rent a small plane. However, when the instructors took Hanjour on three test runs during the second week of August, they found he had trouble controlling and landing the single-engine Cessna 172. The chief flight instructor declined to rent him a plane without more lessons.

An FAA memo, circulated in February 2002, claimed that Suqami stabbed a passenger in Seat 9B, an ex-member of the Israeli Sayeret Matkal. It was based on the frantic phone call of stewardess Betty Ong on AA Flight 11. The FAA and FBI denied the presence of weapons smuggled aboard. Yet Suqami supposedly stabbed the man as he attempted to intervene in the hijacking according to the report.

Suqami's passport was allegedly found near Vesey Street before the towers collapsed. This was mistakenly reported by many news outlets to be Mohamed Atta's passport. A columnist for the Guardian expressed incredulity about the authenticity of this report. It survived the inferno un-singed when the plane's black boxes were never found. They were supposedly found later, however. When the Guardian is doubtful then even they must have problems following the official line.

## Fake Visas

Suqami's passport had a fake visa; facilitated by al Qaeda they said. The passports of Ziad Jarrah and Saeed al Ghamdi were found at the crash site of Flight 93 as well as an air-phone. Some of these passports were likely produced in the UAE or the Jeddah Consulate in Arabia where Mike Springmann has exposed the CIA role at the U.S. Consulate, as he witnessed it near the end of the Reagan era.

According to Springmann, 'the Consulate at Jeddah was the open door through which fifteen of the 9/11 hijackers entered the United States. Since that day, bureaucratic wars and finger-pointing have been the rule in Washington, while the possibility of a full and impartial investigation slowly fades to zero. I have repeatedly been asked by journalists if I believe that the CIA was involved in 9/11.'

As Chief of the Visa Section, he watched scores of visa applicants with no legitimate reason for visiting the US, obtain visas. The CIA was running the consulate, and protests by State Department employees were fruitless. He protested to the top but was eventually sacked.

'The hijackers who obtained visas at Jeddah almost certainly received them courtesy of the CIA. It is likely the visas came along with their services in some U.S. covert operation, probably in Afghanistan. The CIA brings raw recruits from all over the world to learn the finer arts of political murder.' He said 'few Americans understand the pathological Cold War mind set of those who have shaped U.S. foreign policy for over fifty years. For the national security elite, 9/11 was at worst an unfortunate side-effect of business as usual.' His article 'The Hand the Rules the Visa Machine Rocks the World', describing what he saw in Jeddah, was published in Covert Action Quarterly, 2001.

## Double Agents and Destruction

A typical case is Ali Abdul Saoud Mohamed (b.1952) who was a double agent for the CIA and Egyptian Islamic Jihad. He was a translator for Ayman al-Zawahiri (bin Laden's top man), who toured California mosques to raise money to fight the Soviet invasion of Afghanistan. He first entered the CIA office in Cairo and offered his services; they assumed he was an Egyptian spy, and recruited him to be a junior intelligence officer. He was trained by US Special Forces in Special Warfare. In the 1980s he trained anti-Soviet fighters en route to of the US embassies in Nairobi, Kenya and in Dar es Salaam, Tanzania.

In October 2000, he pleaded guilty to five counts of conspiracy to kill US nationals. In addition US military bombs were used. A martial arts expert he spoke fluent English, French, Hebrew and Arabic. He was a major in the Egyptian army's military intelligence unit, discharged for fundamentalism in 1984. By 2006 his sentence had been suspended indefinitely as he was still cooperating with US authorities. His wife said he could not be contacted - he had literally disappeared. He pleaded guilty to bombing the embassies.

It is alleged that Khalid Sheikh Mohammed first suggested the 9/11 plot to bin Laden in 1996 in Afghanistan. This suggests the idea began in 1996, but not in Afghanistan. At that point, bin Laden and al Qaeda were in a period of transition, having just relocated back to Afghanistan from Sudan and Yemen.

The sum of 100,000 dollars was funded to Muhamad Atta's bank account allegedly from the head of Pakistan Intelligence Lt. General Mahmoud Ahmed who met with the CIA and US officials on 9/11. [Leaked by 'The Wall Street Journal']. The Times of India tries to link the Pakistan ISI in with the supposed terrorists and the CIA. Pakistan's spy chief Lt. General Ahmad was in the US when the attacks occurred. He arrived in the US on the 4th of September, a week before the attacks. He had meetings at the

State Department after the attacks on the WTC. But he also had a regular visit of consultations with his US counterparts at the CIA and the Pentagon during the week prior to 9/11.

On the day of 9/11 while Lt. General Ahmad was in the US, the leader of the Northern Alliance Commander Ahmad Shah Masood was assassinated. The Alliance had informed the US that the ISI was implicated in the assassination. The Administration decided in the consultations with Ahmad to cooperate with Pakistan's military intelligence despite its links to the Taliban.

Meanwhile, senior Pentagon and State Department officials had been sent to Islamabad to finalise America's war plans. And on Sunday prior to the onslaught of the bombing of major cities in Afghanistan by the US Air Force on October 7th, Ahmad was sacked from his position as head of the ISI.

## Indian Intelligence

After Ahmad's dismissal the Times of India revealed the links between Ahmad and the assumed leader of the 9/11 attacks, Mohamed Atta. The article was based on an official intelligence report of the Delhi government transmitted to Washington. Agence

France Press confirmed in this regard that: 'The evidence the Government of India have supplied to the US is of a much wider range and depth than just one piece of paper linking a rogue General to some misplaced act of terrorism.'

The Indian intelligence report points to the links between Ahmad and Mohamed Atta. It suggests that the 9/11 attacks were not an act of individual terrorism organised by a separate al Qaeda cell, but rather they were part of coordinated military-intelligence operation.

In judging the alleged links, it could be implied that Lt. General Ahmad as head of the ISI was a US approved appointee. As head of the ISI since 1999, he was in liaison with his US counterparts in the CIA, the Defence Intelligence Agency and the Pentagon. The ISI remained throughout the entire post-Cold War era, the conduit for CIA covert operations in the Caucasus, Central Asia and the Balkans. The Bush Administration was fully cognizant of Ahmad's role. Rather than waging a drive against international terrorism, it would suggest that it was aiding it, using the ISI as a link.

General Ahmed had top secret talks with the Deputy Secretary of State, Richard Armitage on 13/11 who warned him that Pakistan would become an enemy unless it supported the US War on Terror against the Taliban. But he was sacked in October and replaced by a more co-operative head of Pakistan Intelligence.

It is on record that Ahmad was against the US invasion and so the Bush Administration and neo-cons became most influential in his demise. He now teaches holy Islamic doctrine so perhaps it is also a sign of his loyalty to the Islamic cause. Ahmed's role in the whole neo-con deception policy was clandestine. To get Ahmed to return to Afghanistan to get the Taliban to surrender bin Laden was just a feint move on the global chess board, used as a final threat before justifying an invasion.

## Give us Bin Laden or War

On September 13th, Pakistan President Pervez Musharraf confirmed that he would send chief spy Lt. General Ahmad to meet the Taliban and negotiate the extradition of bin Laden. This decision was at Washington's behest, most probably agreed upon during the meeting between Dick Armitage and Ahmed at the State Department. Pakistan's chief spy travels back from Washington to Islamabad. At American urging, Ahmed travelled to Kandahar, Afghanistan. There he demanded bin Laden's surrender without conditions, he told Taliban leader Mohammad Omar, or face certain war with the United States and its allies.

Ahmed's meetings on two separate missions with the Taliban were reported as a failure. Yet this failure to extradite Osama was part of Washington's design, providing a pretext for a military intervention which was already in the pipeline. If bin Laden had been extradited, the main justification for waging a war against global terrorism would fade. And the evidence suggests that this war had been planned well in advance of 9/11, in response to broad strategic and economic objectives.

# CHAPTER 9

## The Towers

*Philippe Petit tight roped back and forth between the twin towers as soon as they were built. The police arrested him and let him go when the people said he was a hero. He proved that at least he could get passed security and health and safety without insurance and provide free entertainment into the bargain.*

The Tower of Babel forms the focus of a story told in the Book of Genesis of the Bible. According to the story, a united humanity of the generations following the Great Flood, speaking a single language and migrating from the east came to the land of Shinar. The King James Version of the Bible gives us: And they said, Go to, let us build us a city and a tower, whose top may reach unto heaven; and let us make us a name, lest we be scattered abroad upon the face of the whole earth. And the Lord came down to see the city and the tower, which the children of men builded.

And the Lord said, Behold, the people is one, and they have all one language; and this they begin to do: and now nothing will be restrained from them, which they have imagined to do. Go to, let us go down, and there confound their language, that they may not understand one another's speech. So the Lord scattered them abroad from thence upon the face of all the earth: and they left off to build the city. Therefore is the name of it called Babel; because the Lord did there confound the language of all the earth and from thence did the Lord scatter them abroad upon the face of all the earth. - Genesis 11:4–9.

And they began to build, and in the fourth week they made brick with fire, and the bricks served them for stone, and the clay with which they cemented them together was asphalt which comes out of the sea, and out of the fountains of water in the land of Shinar. And they built it: forty and three years were they building it; its breadth was 203 bricks, and the height of a brick was the third of one; its height amounted to 5433 cubits and two palms, and the extent of one wall was thirteen stades and of the other thirty stades. - Jubilees 10:20-21.(6).

## Secret Arts

Some months prior to 9/11, drawings and videos were made by Austrian art students having access to the 91$^{st}$ floor of the North Tower. They hired a helicopter to film the 'B thing', possibly a figure, one day. They had built up scores of cardboard boxes as an enclosed passage to an open window; and built a contraption known as the Trojan to project from the window. The window pane was removed by a tradesman overnight and replaced later. The students were using a safety harness to walk out on this Trojan platform, extending several feet outside the window.

Their drawings include the structure at the 91$^{st}$ floor with projection lines going up from the lift shafts. It shows the two hundred and forty perimeter columns including the four major corner columns. It also shows most of the 47 core columns and the lifts. They had a VCR set up. A helicopter is shown of a scheduled flight at 6.20; 6.23; and 6.27a.m. This was likely for three trips around the tower. One person would likely be filmed on the platform. They took precautions and worked at night and hired a lawyer for some reason, until completion, when their story was covered in the NY Times on Aug18/01.

# Credentials

The Twin Towers in New York were 1360 feet high and designed by Minoru Yamasaki as lead architect and Emery Roth & Sons as associate architects. And like the more classical and illustrious Babel was destined to fulfil a catastrophic prophesy, such is the power of Oligarchs in the world.

A former CIA and civilian pilot has sworn an affidavit, stating that no planes flew into the Twin Towers as it would have been physically impossible. John Lear, the son of the Lear jet inventor Bill Lear, has given his expert evidence that it would have been physically impossible for Boeings, like Flights AA11 and UA175 to have hit the Twin Towers on 9/11.

He stated that: 'No Boeing 767 airliners hit the Twin Towers as fraudulently alleged by the government, media and the National Institute for Science and Technology and its contractors. Such crashes did not occur because they are physically impossible as depicted, for the following reasons:

In the case of UA 175 going into the South Tower, a real Boeing 767 would have begun telescoping when the nose hit the fourteen inch wide steel columns which are thirty nine inches on centre, typical. The vertical and horizontal tail would have instantaneously separated from the aircraft then hit the steel box columns and fallen to the ground. The engines when impacting the steel columns would have maintained their general shape and either fallen to the ground or been recovered in the debris of the collapsed building.

No Boeing 767 could attain a speed of 540 mph at 1000 feet above sea level as parasite drag doubles with velocity and parasite power cubes with velocity. The fan portion of the engine is not designed to accept the volume of dense air at that altitude and speed. The piece of alleged external fuselage containing the window cut outs is inconsistent with an airplane that hit the steel box columns. It would have crumpled.

No significant part of the Boeing 767 or engine could have penetrated the fourteen inch steel columns and thirty seven feet beyond the massive core of the tower without part of it falling to the ground. The debris of the collapse should have contained massive sections of the Boeing 767, including the engine cores weighing approximately nine thousand pounds apiece which could not have been hidden. Yet there is no evidence of any of these massive structural components from either 767 at the WTC. Such complete disappearance of 767's is impossible.'

## Artefacts

On 9/11 the remains of a gear/drive shaft mechanism was found on the ground. An engine part marked CFM56 or CF6 made by General Electric was found on Murray St. This was secured by the FBI and an aircraft wheel was also taped off by the FBI. A Boeing uses Pratt & Whitney, General Electric or Rolls Royce engines. This part was identified by another source as being a Pratt & Whitney High Pressure Turbine Stage 1 Cooling Duct Assembly Part No JT9D-7A/7F/7J from a Boeing 747 not a 767. Also a very large section of an aircraft fuselage was found and photographed on the flat roof of a nearby financial building. This was the part John Lear said was suspect.

## Design

Both technical calculations and testimony from WTC structural engineers confirm that the Twin Towers were built to withstand the impact from the passenger jets that hit them on 9/11. Airplane impact tests conducted by WTC structural engineers during the design of the Twin Towers used the Boeing 707, which was one of the largest passenger jets in the world at the time.

The results of the test, carried out early in 1964, calculated that the towers would handle the impact of a 707 travelling at speed without collapsing. Even though the two Boeing 767 aircraft that were said to be used in the 9/11 attacks were slightly larger than the 707, technical comparisons show that the 707 has more destructive force at cruising speed.

The maximum take-off weight for a Boeing 707-320B is 336,000 pounds. The maximum take-off weight for a Boeing 767-200ER is 395,000 pounds. The wingspan of a Boeing 707 is 146 feet. The wingspan of a Boeing 767 is 156 feet. The length of a Boeing 707 is 153 feet. The length of a Boeing 767 is 159 feet. The Boeing 707 could carry 23,000 gallons of fuel. The Boeing 767 could carry 23,980 gallons of fuel. The cruise speed of a Boeing 707 is 607 mph = 890 ft. /s. The cruise speed of a Boeing 767 is 530 mph = 777 ft. /s.

We can now calculate the energy that the plane would impart to the towers in any accidental collision. The kinetic energy released by a Boeing 707 at cruise speed is:

KE = 0.5 x 336,000 x (890) ^2/32.174 = 4.136 billion ft. lbs force equivalent to 5,607,720 Kilojoules.

The kinetic energy released by a Boeing 767 at cruise speed is:

KE = 0.5 x 395,000 x (777) ^2/32.174 = 3.706 billion ft. lbs force equivalent to 5,024,650 Kilojoules.

So there is not much difference, depending on their speeds. The difference in energy is mainly due to the difference in their cruise velocities that is magnified by the square of these velocities. According to John Lear it is impossible for a Boeing to travel at these speeds at this low altitude in any case. The fan portion of the engine is not designed to accept the volume of dense air at that altitude and speed.

When interviewed in 1993, Lead WTC Structural Engineer John Skilling told The Seattle Times: 'He was rightfully confident that neither the impact of a large passenger jet nor the ensuing office fires was capable of bringing down the Twin Towers. The main problem would be the fuel from the airplane would dump into the building. There would be a fire and some people would be killed but the building structure would still be there.'

The towers were designed to survive multiple plane crashes. This assertion is supported by Frank De Martini, the on-site construction manager for the World Trade Centre, who said on January 25, 2001: 'The building was designed to have a fully loaded 707 crash into it. I believe that the building could sustain multiple impacts of jetliners because this structure is like the mosquito netting on your screen door - this intense grid - and the jet plane is just a pencil puncturing that screen netting. It really does nothing to the screen netting.'

De Martini appeared to be so confident that the towers would not collapse that he stayed behind, after the airplane impacts, to help some people. De Martini risked his life to save others, but the evidence suggests that he did not think he was endangering himself by going back into the building.

## Structure

If you clap hands one hundred and ten times (110 floors) very fast and time it, it's impossible to do it in ten or eleven seconds the time it took the towers to fall at near free fall speed - that is at practically zero resistance. The free fall time would be 9.2 seconds. The Twin Towers were constructed to withstand Earthquakes, Hurricane winds and Boeing or Jet aircraft impacts. The outer structure was basically a close knit lattice network of 240 steel columns, including four massive corner columns, and lateral Vierendeel floor trusses. The 47 huge core columns started from the bedrock six or seven stories below ground level. The trusses were resistant to multi-directional forces such as twisting or torque being of a cubic open web structure. The core and perimeter steel columns were typically at least fourteen inches wide (7) consisting of boxed and triplex geometry of solid steel sections, separated by twenty two inch wide window frames in the perimeter; above the tree frame base structure (8).

Each floor consisted of steel reinforced, four inch thick lightweight concrete set onto pre-fabricated steel sheets supported by the trusses. The high-strength; load-bearing Vierendeel trusses were spaced closely together to form a strong, rigid wall structure, supporting all lateral loads such as wind loads, and sharing the gravity load with the core and perimeter columns. The perimeter structure was constructed with extensive use of prefabricated modular pieces each consisting of bolted columns.

The spandrel plates were welded to the columns to create the modular pieces off-site. At each level was the central rectangle 135 by 87 feet, the core, containing the forty seven steel columns running from the bedrock to the top of the tower. The large space between the perimeter and core was bridged by the floor trusses. Adjacent column modules were bolted together with the splices in series between the spandrels. The spandrel plates were located at every floor on alternative columns, transmitting shear stress between columns, allowing them to work together in resisting lateral loads.

The joints between modules were staggered vertically so the column splices between adjacent modules were not at the same floor. The core of the towers housed the elevator and utility shafts, restrooms, three stairwells, and other support spaces. The core floors supported their own weight as well as live loads, providing lateral stability to the exterior walls and distributing wind loads among the exterior walls. The floors of lightweight concrete were laid on a fluted steel deck. The grid of lightweight bridging trusses and main trusses supported the floors.

The trusses connected to the perimeter at alternate columns and were on six foot and eight inch centres (apart). The top chords of the trusses were bolted to seats welded to the spandrels on the exterior side and channel welded to the core columns on the interior side. The floors were connected to the perimeter spandrel plates with viscoelastic dampers that helped reduce the amount of sway felt by building occupants.

Hat trusses or outriggers were located from the 107th floor to the top of the buildings and were designed to support a tall communication antenna on top of each building. Only the North Tower had an antenna fitted, added circa 1972/3 or later (9). The truss system consisted of six trusses along the long axis of the core and four along the short axis. This truss system allowed some load redistribution between the perimeter and core columns and supported the transmission tower.

The tube frame design using steel core and perimeter columns protected with sprayed-on fire resistant material created a relatively lightweight structure. This would sway more in response to the wind compared to traditional structures such as the Empire State Building that have thick, heavy masonry for fireproofing of steel structural elements. During the design process, wind tunnel tests were done to establish design wind pressures that the World Trade Centre towers could be subjected to and structural response to those forces.

Experiments were done to evaluate how much sway occupants could comfortably tolerate, however, many subjects experienced dizziness and other ill effects. One of the chief engineers Leslie Robertson had worked with the Canadian engineer Alan G. Davenport to develop the viscoelastic dampers in order to absorb some of the sway. These viscoelastic dampers were used throughout the structure at the joints between floor trusses and perimeter columns together with some other structural modifications.

In 1973, EPA banned spray-applied surfacing asbestos-containing material for fireproofing and insulating purposes. The steel columns had been coated with asbestos well over half way up on both towers and had to be terminated. The cost of removing it in 2001 would have been $200 million and the towers were losing business finding it hard to let office space.

Since the 1993 bombing of the Trade Center, it is unlikely that many companies would want to become new tenants. And the Health and Safety laws regarding asbestos may have made the owners - NY Port of Authority vulnerable to litigation from full occupancy at some later stage. There is evidence that the top floors were never fully occupied, if they had any ceilings.

Thousands of bolts and welds cannot fail simultaneously in a reinforced structure, unless severed by explosives. If the plane explosion caused localised red heat the steel would have cooled within minutes. A simple analogy is the forging of steel in a blacksmith's hearth to white heat, it just tempers the steel. It was an hour before so called collapse and the firemen said the fires were under control. The Madrid Windsor Tower in 2005 burned like a raging inferno for twenty four hours yet it did not collapse. Indeed no high rise building as ever collapsed from fire damage.

## Mist & Sunder

The National Institute of Standards and Technology (NIST) released nearly 500 pages of documents, detailing the latest findings of its investigation of the WTC collapses on 9/11. These include its hypotheses for the collapse sequences of each of the Twin Towers; details of their analysis of interviews with nearly 1,200 building occupants, emergency responders, and victims' relatives; and information from their analysis of the emergency response and evacuation procedures. Their investigation into the collapses is based upon an analysis of thousands of photos and videos, examination of many of the elements used to construct the towers, and computer-enhanced modelling of the plane impacts and the spreading of the fires. Their hypothesis is that the towers collapsed ultimately due to the fires they suffered: As the fires burned, the buildings' steel core columns buckled and shortened. This shifted more load to the buildings' perimeter columns, which were already affected by the heat of the fires, and caused them to give way under the increased stress. Investigators have conducted a test with a reconstructed section of the WTC floor, and found that the original fireproofing was sufficient to meet the New York City building code.

They say that had a typical office fire occurred in the towers, without the structural damage and the loss of some fireproofing caused by the plane impacts, it is likely the buildings would have remained standing. Lead investigator Dr Shyam Sunder says, "The buildings performed as they should have in the airplane impact and extreme fires to which they were subjected. There is nothing there that stands out as abnormal." NIST's theories of why the WTC buildings collapsed conflict with an earlier investigation by FEMA, which claimed the collapse of the North Tower had begun in its core, rather than its perimeter columns. [National Institute of Standards and Technology, 10/19/2004; New York Times10/20/2004].[Source: History Commons].

Sunder concludes the buildings performed as they should have. This statement apart from being insane, suggests that all tall buildings in the world might be liable to collapse in less than ten seconds should there be structural damage and extreme fires, without total fire proofing. Yet WTC 7 fell in six seconds but it was not hit by a plane.

## The Metallurgy of Severed Steel

Dust samples examined by Professor Stephen Jones contained 6% spheroids of iron, with sulphur and barium particles as confirmed by scanning electron microscope, XRF and atomic absorption analysis. This indicated the possible use of military grade thermite known as Nano - thermite causing melting and blowing of molten steel into the air, forming spherical droplets. The detonation of placed charges was likely initiated by remote radio control as a standard procedure, as wiring would have been very difficult and easily traced.

Pictures at ground zero show several base box columns that were clean cut through at near forty five degree angles The steel had to be severed on all the major core columns for symmetrical collapse otherwise any resilient column structure would cause a turning force contributing to a more random or asymmetrical collapse.

## Cause

The evidence given in '9/11: Explosive Evidence - Experts Speak Out' demonstrates clearly that pre-planted explosives - not jet plane impacts and fires - destroyed the Twin Towers. The WTC designers were correct in their analysis in the 1960s, and the evidence that these buildings were brought down by explosive demolition corroborates their conclusions.

There was no official explanation for WTC 7 falling which had minor damage from fires. The evidence for WTC 7 confirms planted explosives and controlled demolition. Initially at least four floors were blown out with window fires, and the basement floors were severed well before demolition at 5.20 p.m. Michael Hess, head of OEM was allegedly with Barry Jennings that day. Barry said they experienced an explosion in the building long before its collapse. He said they were trapped between the 6th and 8th floors at one stage indicating a stairway had collapsed.

In order to bring the twin towers down in perfect symmetry would require placing cutter or concussion charges, in a symmetrical pattern, on the base columns and the core columns. The core base columns were likely severed at the same time as the initial 'plane' strike. The perimeter column structure was weakened by cutting the massive corner columns at several levels. Total collapse could then be initiated in a rapid synchronised relay starting from the top proceeding as an ignition sequence in the core.

The severing of the major core columns in the towers using concussion explosives would collapse the core and disintegrate the building. Access to the massive core columns would be a more covert operation and effectively accomplished from inside the lift shafts during night work; thereby limiting the more extensive stripping work required for placing all of the charges needed for the usual implosion methods.

It was observed on film that the corner columns were cut at several critical points using exothermic incendiaries. White hot steel was seen pouring out from a corner column at the 81$^{st}$ floor. This would have severed the top section of the towers at four major seats of failure thus initiating the collapse, starting at the top. Then this process was likely repeated in the remaining two major sections. A progression of consecutive floor collapse was seen as puffs or squibs progressing all the way down in advance, followed by the exploding structure and dust, in the final nine seconds.

## Witnesses

In all the three towers the first evidence from firemen, newscasters and film and scores of witnesses hearing secondary explosions, causing rising dust and smoke clouds. The janitor in the North Tower, William Rodriguez stated he heard a loud boom in the basement below him and an upward air draught then about six seconds later he heard another explosion way above him, at the same time the plane supposedly hit. He said he was in sub-basement level one.

At the same time it is alleged, two workers were injured - one Felipe David and Salvatore Giambango were in a lower sub level. David said he saw a fire ball and dropped to the floor with severe face and hand burns. Another Jose Sanches working in sub level four also witnessed the fire ball. There were others who witnessed hearing a major explosion in the sub-basement. Tony Saltalamacchia said he heard a massive explosion in the basement then ten more explosions higher up in the building. Hursley Lever was in sub—basement four when he was hit by the fire ball and was injured.

## Film Makers

The French Naudet brothers Jules and Gedeon were guests of the local Engine 7 Ladder 1 Station Precinct at 100 Duane St doing a film covering a rookie called Tony Benetatos with James Hanlon, an actor and probationer fireman, since July. They spent the night at the station and Jules cooked a French supper. The next day the crew were called out to a gas leak in a street manhole and they arrived there at about eight thirty a.m.

It was Battery Chief Joseph Pfeifer who tested the manhole cover whilst being filmed, after the first fireman had tested it. Then suddenly there is a sound of a plane and they look up to see it hit the North Tower. The first image of impact is perfectly in focus but then zooms out of focus as if out of control.

After the filming of this unique incident Jules went with Pfeiffer in a fire engine to film the exclusive footage of the first fire crew - Engine Seven to arrive at the North Tower. Gedeon followed later on foot taking film of people looking up at the tower and recording some of the comments of people seeing the second plane striking the South Tower.

## Questions

That this was a staged event we have to raise the following questions of chance and reason. The Street of the leak was at Lispenard St. and Church St. with the Twin Towers in full view several blocks away. The camera looks at the testing of the leak by Pfeifer only moments before the plane arrives and fortunately is able to locate the source of the sound and catch the plane on film before hitting the tower. The camera is able to focus on the reactions of the firemen before scanning to locate a plane within two or three seconds of the sound. It then 'locates the plane' suddenly appearing between other buildings 'moving at about 260 yards per second' before hitting the tower. This must have been accomplished by using two cameras, one already set up facing the towers.

There are many more unique coincidences that cannot be explained other than the Naudet film was set up in the foreknowledge of the time and exact location of the event. And this event was that an explosion in the North Tower would occur at 8.46 am but not by an aircraft hitting the tower.

Jules Naudet travelled with Chief Pfeifer and was first into the North Tower yet none of the team of Engine Seven /Ladder 1 suffered any casualties but other Engines allegedly lost men. The losses to the FDNY is large enough to question the authenticity of the data, let alone the total figure of 343, particularly as the SSA appear not to have any records of these deaths on the MDF files.

Pfeiffer's ladder was the first into the North Tower and Jules filmed the crew and showed the lobby windows were all blown out. They said the cause of this was a fireball from the jet fuel that blew down one of the central elevator shafts, disabling all the lifts. Also one of the firemen is saying he saw the second plane hit the South Tower.

The most likely cause of the lobby damage would be the result of a powerful ground tremor caused by high explosive blasts in the severing of the basement columns i.e. a shock wave, since the rest of the lobby appeared dust laden with no sign of fire damage, albeit cracks in the walls.

At one stage the elevator opened and several people walked out as if bemused and walking along seemingly unconcerned through the lobby to exit the place. So that one lift was still working as the doors had opened. In the lobby the fire Chief stated the fire was above the 78th floor but this was inaccurate. It was at the 93rd to 99th floors and they said it would take a fireman with sixty pounds of equipment one minute per flight to get up there since all the lifts were defunct. They would not easily get back down in time. Fortunately none of Engine Seven crew lost their lives in the making of the film. The lifts could not have been damaged at all.

## A Greek Tragedy

For the people trapped above the 91st floor many were unable to get down so they made their way to the top only to find the exit doors were locked. About two hundred were trapped and soaked in water from the fire sprinklers according to the media. Many others hung out of the windows to escape the fire, heat and smoke. But it can now be proven that these cases did not happen and indeed we have video close ups of the fake people in the windows and close ups of the 'jumpers'.

The recording of a 9/11 operator to a lady victim was tragic when listening to her desperate pleas for help to which she replied - be calm the firemen are near. Eventually they appeared to jump to their deaths on film. All of the photographs of the jumpers on magnification are seen to be fake with pixels deformed in the outlines of the cut and paste images.

Some of the jumpers were holding hands, others - an estimated sixty feet away from the building. One was precisely upside down with his hands behind his head - in a seemingly relaxed mode. And the videos of the people in the windows show obvious deformed and elongated arms that become macabre distortions when moving. The windows were sealed units of toughened glass yet the people were hanging and standing and leaning out of them; and quite a task to break many sealed toughened glass windows and clear out the jagged glass. In relation to the scale of the widows these images of people were about 7 feet tall.

## Ready to Rescue

On 9/11 there were rescue teams at hand from both military and civilian volunteers who were ready to fly helicopters to the top but an FAA order was given for them to stand down. There was really no one to be rescued. Access to the roof had been locked ever since the 1993 bombing. Instead, the idea was to show graphic images of people forced to jump as evidence of people trapped in the North Tower. One fire-fighter called Chief Palmer who had got to the 78th floor of the South Tower reported to Battalion Seven that the fires were under control.

Genelle Guzman-McMillan gave a fantastic story that she was buried when the North Tower fell. She had got down to the 13th from the 64th floor with her friend Rose. She was trapped as the 'stair case curled around her' whilst falling to ground. She was buried under rubble for 27 hours and was finally rescued. A man named Paul held her left hand that was sticking out of the concrete, steel and rubble until rescued. The rescuers finally dug her out but she never saw Paul again. She said it was a miracle and it turned her life back to God. She was the last person to be rescued.

## Location of Flight UA175

Recent investigations from the Pilots for Truth since 2006 have obtained startling evidence that Flight No 175 Tail No. N612 UA was located within fifty miles of Pittsburgh, Pa at 9.23 Eastern Time according to a standard message sent by the despatcher - Ed Ballinger. The pilot did not reply to this plain language message: Message from CHIDD - Beware any cockpit intrusion: Two Aircraft in NY. Hit Trade Centre Buids... CHIDD Ed Ballinger.

However the ACARS system (used since 1978) automatically relayed back: 09111323 108575 0574. Like e/mails this ACK message is always given if message received, at bottom of the sent message within the minute. Thus it means 0911 date at 1323Z time (GMT) or 9.23 a.m. Eastern Daylight Time, followed by identity code 108575 0574 data was received. There is no chance the plane could return the signal if its electronic circuits are cut. The only data saved is in the Black Box which for example can be located later by a radar bleep signal.

Four messages were sent from Chicago etc. by Jerry Tsen, Ad Rogers and Ed Ballinger at 8:59(JT); 9.03 (EB); 9.03 (AR); and 9.23 (EB). The first three were routed through Middleton (MDT), Harrisburg, Pa.

The last one through (PIT) Pittsburgh Int. Airport (Approx: 350 miles from NY). Remember 9.03 was the time Flight 175UA allegedly hit the South Tower. Since the radar automatically tracks the aircraft from the Central Processing System and selects the strongest signal by re-routing through the nearest ground station the plane must have been heading west in a line parallel and north of Harrisburg to Pittsburgh at this time. The ACARS system ensures that if a plane changes its course at any time the CPS is tracking it and can always acknowledge a message unless lost at sea, crashed or other otherwise disabled.

## Moral Witnesses

Dr Rowan Williams, a bishop of Wales, was just a block or so away from the plaza on 9/11. He is said to have told an airline pilot in the immediate aftermath of the atrocity that God had not prevented it because He has given humans free will. He and others had to escape their dust filled building and helped to evacuate a group of young children. They got to a porta - cabin and a workman inside offered up a prayer. The following year he became Archbishop of Canterbury Cathedral and spiritual leader of the Anglican Church.

Dr Williams said the West should not retaliate. The Rev. Peter Mullen berates Williams for having the sentiment of Jesus. Mullen was worried about the Archbishop's attitude to the war on Islamic terror. Mullen said there was confusion here between revenge and justice. 'While I may seek follow the teaching of Christ, I must not do this on behalf of those who have suffered innocently. It is my duty to take up the sword on behalf of the fatherless children and the widow. This would concede victory to the aggressors who silenced more than 3,000 of us on 9/11 - and they have threatened to do worse. He must be glad to be getting out of all this. This very nice man and hairy leftie is so benign, kindly and learned, just the qualifications for the mastership of a Cambridge college.'

These are the hypocritical if not political words of Dr Mullen. The very essence of Christianity is charity not revenge. Dr Mullen might seek for justice in his own vengeful God, who is not like Christ but more like the vengeful God in the Old Testament. And Dr Williams was right after all.

Whether for truth, or for lies and infamy, the pen is mightier than the sword. According to the Assyrian sage Ahiqar, 7th century BC - 'The word is mightier than the sword.'

# CHAPTER 10

## *Illusion*

*The magician fools his audience by two means. First he gains their confidence. Then he tricks them out of it as fast as the hand deceives the eye.*

It was to be the greatest illusive hoax of any century, images that fool the idle eye and by special effects based on media craft and years of experience. The tricks of 9/11 were based on previous ideas but with little experience of this new type of event.

There were however recent similar events using explosives, the only major difference would be the aircraft. But that was the big illusion - there were no Boeing planes hitting buildings - it was nearly all video fakery with the support of the major TV networks. They also had the resources of many combined skills and the power to control the people's collective mind.

And any questions might mean possible ruin to the whistle blowers.

The most striking paradox of the towers' destruction was the complete absence of any remains either of body parts or office fabrications and contents. An audit might give 60,000 phones, 40,000 steel chairs, 30,000 desks and steel cabinets, computers and acres of carpets. This lot simply cannot be turned into dust by fire or explosions. There is no other possible explanation other than the buildings were empty of people and parts.

The only evidence of office stationary was the thousands of paper sheets - nothing else left but silicate particulates, cable wire, ducting, pipes and steel structure. This in itself is the evidence that indicates the buildings had been emptied prior to demolition as per the normal procedure for such a task. Experts say that detonation by remote control is expensive but does not require wiring procedures but is more prone to signal failure.

So how was the real footage of explosions faked to include the planes striking the buildings at the same instant in such a short time available? Well indeed the time factor was critical for several mistakes were revealed, in their satanic haste. The key is video compositing - objects can be inserted into a live replay.

Indeed a brilliant 9/11 researcher Alex Baker gives a definitive thesis on how the fakers and the takers did it and how they failed to match up the various images. He explains how and why the various shots do not match. And he reproduces the CNN Hezerkhani video with another fake plane - his own computer generated image, showing his superimposed image doing exact same ghost entry motions as Hezerkhani's image, in tandem. The CNN footage shows a plane entering a tower with no immediate damage, either to the plane or the tower. The idea was to make the fake plane go through the building otherwise they would have to simulate a plane crashing and breaking up

and falling back into the streets below. This would not have been possible to simulate at the time and also to plant all the debris including massive titanium engines. According to Mr. Baker:

'A layer mask is a video software tool which allows one area in a video to become transparent, making any video object which enters this layer mask area invisible. A false airplane image escaping a layer mask is the only reasonable explanation for the 'nose out' observation in the Fox Chopper 5 video. Based on my research, a video technician faded the picture to black after realizing the nose of a false airplane image escaped the layer mask. The Chopper 5 footage was never replayed, indicating mens rea (a guilty mind). The Chopper 5 footage was replaced on the official government archive with completely different footage.'

Three of the live shots - ABC Chopper 7, Fox Chopper 5 and WIPX - of the plane were recorded at the time of impact. They show the plane disappearing behind the towers but not the impact itself. The most obvious mistake was that of the Fox 5 image showing the plane literally going through the South Tower, such that a perfect image of its nose emerges in exactly the same shape as before it entered.

Baker superimposed the two images of pre-entry and exit showing they were identical. This particular clip was not shown again by the Fox media giant but a re-constructed (doctored) version continued to be shown, with the broken nose in flames just as if it was part of exploding debris. Other networks showed it but they covered up the miscreant nose with their logos. However it did not stop the anchor men saying the plane had gone right through the building!

Few objects can travel through any kind of thick steel structure unless travelling above 1 km per second (the speed of a bullet) such as high explosive charges that blast through, by cutting the steel at up to 20 km per second. The force is proportional to the square of this velocity. Depleted Uranium shells can do this more effectively because of their combined mass, velocity, hardness and sharpness e.g. to penetrate thickened steel sections of tanks. Aviation fuel explosions have a much lower velocity of 100 metres per second.

Image screening is a technique - using the Luma key. In video editing, luminance keying is setting the brightness level and all brighter or darker pixels from the set level are turned off and will be transparent. A second clip or image can be inserted behind to show where the pixels have been turned off. Luminance keying is used when working with grayscale images. A number of live conditions are required, such as high contrast between the foreground subject (the towers) and a bright sky background. This is obvious when comparing the live shots of no planes with the washed out background of the doctored images showing the fake planes. Also there must be no camera tilting, zooming or panning and a stationary position.

What happened with Fox Chopper Five to cause the mistake? The layer compositing uses three layers with the centre layer showing an image of the plane effectively travelling across the screen and slowing down in the last frames. The plane layer has a mask splitting the screen vertically to prevent the plane's image travelling past the real edge of the tower.

The operator Kai Simonson for Fox News was contracted as a Video Compositor expert to fly in Chopper Five. He had to hold the camera steady in line with the tower using a gyro mount. The plane then suddenly appears to the right of the tower in a few frames before entering the tower. Video frame speeds are normally 30 frames per second. If the camera moves laterally too quickly or say if the helicopter drifted too fast to the left, the mask moves past the real image of the tower's edge and exposes the image of the nose of the plane as if exiting the tower i.e. the camera's mask has moved beyond the edge of the tower. Thus according to Mr. Baker again:

'Making an airplane image disappear through a wall is done by masking. A shape can simply be drawn, defining a region of transparency. As the airplane image crosses into the mask, it disappears. However, the positioning and timing are critical. Misplacing the mask or the airplane image by even a few pixels or having an explosion go too early would be a dead giveaway. Compositors would not even contemplate trying to show a plane hitting the tower wall in real-time. How convenient it was that all of the 9/11 news helicopters, including Chopper Five and Chopper Seven, were positioned north and west of the towers. None could see the plane hit the wall United flight 175 allegedly crashed into, in the live shots that morning.

News helicopter cameras are mounted in a mechanical gyroscope stabilizer system. Though the helicopter is vibrating and unsteady, the helicopter video system is remarkably stable. Trying to real-time composite the smooth motion of an airplane onto any sort of non-stabilized shot is futile. Neither of the two Fox News camera operators followed the motion of the incoming airplane until it was close to the tower.

Inserting an airplane image into a live shot needs the camera to be still. Zooming, panning, tilting, or focusing during the shot would reveal the composite right away, because the airplane image would not be synchronized with the camera's motion images. Compositing onto a moving camera shot is possible, with a system called 'motion tracking', but not in real-time. Real-time motion tracking did not exist in 2001.

When United 175 appears on the screen, both Chopper Five and Chopper Seven are as still as possible, drifting slowly to the left. As soon as the plane is gone, both camera operators tilt and pan the camera around. News helicopters are moving around all the time. They zoom in and out, pan left and right, tilt up and down, normally. They would follow an incoming passenger jet. It's not possible for all of the compositional characteristics required for real-time compositing to happen on both live airplane shots, during the exact time the airplanes are on screen.'

Simonson's reply to Baker regarding how a plane could penetrate a building intact was: How do you know it could not penetrate the tower since this was an entirely new event? The man blagged in the face of common sense, let alone scientific knowledge. It is true that one engine of a B25 bomber did pass through the Empire State building in 1945 but not the rest of the plane's structure which crumpled. The second engine penetrated to the lift shaft.

Video-mania: Scores of different faked videos from different angles were selected to go live hours later from the networks and amateurs alike e.g. Michael Hezarkhani (for CNN) an LA diamond merchant; Evan Fairbanks (for ABC); and Gamma Press (which also showed the nose penetrate the South Tower) and the Naudet films. In the Fairbanks video the hysterical voice overs were not included in the live showing... Holy Sh.. etc. but kept in later for the video release. Fairbanks said the FBI had asked him to edit it out. But later he said it was because the mike had been switched off for the live Fox studio version.

At least seventy clips of the media, professionals and amateurs were either filmed on the day or, most of them were developed and offered for public use and trade later. These can be seen on numerous websites. Note the number of press helicopters hovering around that day and the numerous other geographic sites e.g. tops of tall buildings that were already set up with cameras for the event. However Chopper 5 of Fox News was five miles away in New Jersey as Kai Simonson switched to zoom on cue.

We even have a Russian cameraman flying down the Hudson in a Cessna taking film. Many of the arrangers of these clips do not support the conspiracy theorists. Nevertheless they do give much detail as supplied by the various researchers that is a genuine effort to give unbiased accounts of the source materials and their participants. Even so any explanations offered avoid controversy by the excessive use of secondary related data. But they do mention the videos that were obviously faked.

In WABC for example it was Peter Jennings the veteran stalwart with insight who stated accurately: 'Anybody who ever watched a building being demolished on purpose knows that if you're going to do this you have to get at the under infrastructure of a building and bring it down.' Then Don Dahler quickly 'explained' his colleague's oversight: 'It looked like the top part of the building was so weakened by the fire that the weight of it just collapsed the rest of the building, that's what appeared to happen. I did not see anything happening at the base of the building. It all appeared to start at the top and then just collapse the rest of the building by the sheer weight of the top.' Note that he made a point out of not seeing smoke rising from the base, which is undeniable in the video; the one cloud is white and another is sandy yellow coloured.

In the CBS -1 video image there is an effort to explain how the aircraft behaves like a dive bomber, due to seeing it from a different perspective. Thus to any rational mind the question is how does a single event trigger scores of film makers within sixteen minutes, including hiring of planes and helicopters, to be ready exactly on cue to film a second event that happened nearby. No matter how you look at it, with the timing and overwhelming number of fake videos, it points to a staged event.

The Naudet film was pre-planned to the minute knowing the exact time the explosion in the North Tower would occur. It was then edited overnight in which the fake plane was included, so we can see there would be no reason to include having to use a drone. In any case the drone would have to be an explosive missile in itself. And a drone, if it did have the wingspan for the cut outs made, could not cut the steel into straight geometric patterns. The pattern of the cut outs clearly shows the columns were severed laterally in a regular stepped sequence; the shiny alloy cladding breaking away from the steel at lateral joints, indicating that the cutting process was precisely arranged to give an apparent but crude outline of a giant wing span of a plane.

Social Security

The illusion becomes seriously less bleak and more hopeful with recent checks into the death tally on 9/11. It would appear that death rates in both NY State and New Jersey did not increase above normal that day. More notable was that in random samples of supposed victims of 9/11 not one was found on the Death Master File. No full explanation has so far been given by the Social Security Administration except sometimes certain names may be undisclosed for various reasons. Usually however all deaths are recorded when SSA is advised either by family or state authorities. An official enquiry into this anomaly had begun after a news bulletin.

Thomas Hargrove of Scripps Howard News Service: July 9, 2011.Washington. A New York congresswoman who represents Manhattan wants answers to why nearly 3,000 victims of the 9/11 terrorists' attacks weren't reported in the Social Security Administration's official list of deceased Americans. Carolyn Maloney said her staff made inquiries after the errors in the federal Death Master File were detected by Scripps Howard News Service. The file is a public record intended to protect families of the deceased from identity theft and other types of fraud.

'While nearly 3,000 individuals were killed on 9/11, the list does not show an increase in numbers from the typical DMF daily average,' Maloney said. 'A sampling of those names did not yield any matches in the DMF and confirms their apparent absence.'

This then also throws much doubt into the number of firemen killed which was said to be 343. If we consider that Engine Seven who were the first team to arrive at the North Tower lost no-one, yet were inside the building and were trying to get up to the

93 rd. floor we must assume they were extremely lucky. Other teams also arrived there and apparently lost lives, including NY Fire Chief Peter Ganci after the North Tower finally collapsed. The toll of firemen deaths taken from one particular source gave a partial tally of 95 deaths for six battalions. Even this has to be seriously questioned since no evidence of these deaths is recorded by the SSA.

## Preparations

To carry out preparation for a standard demolition, the buildings would normally have to be empty for at least a week, or two. However there had been reconstruction work going on in the towers from the 78th floor upwards some time before 9/11. In addition there was a 36 hour power down at the weekend prior to 9/11; and there had been an 'evacuation drill' an hour beforehand. It seems there had been a power down from early Saturday morning till Sunday afternoon. There were workmen or electricians in the buildings according to Scott Forbes. His office was on the 97th floor and he said they had been given three weeks' notice. In the experience of the company a power down had not happened before. He didn't go to work on the Tuesday. A number of unidentified vans were recorded, by Intelligence agents, arriving in the early mornings for ten days prior to 9/11 according to Susan Lindauer, a CIA asset.

The core was the key to the structure's strength and its columns were part of the initial major seats of failure and accessible from inside the lift shafts. Otherwise it is usually necessary to remove floor and wall fabrics, like tiling, carpets and plaster, to gain access to the columns and to aid in a symmetrical collapse; and to ensure the removal of all objects that would become missiles.

However this was not a normal implosion procedure but a series of powerful explosions raining down massive girders as far as the Winter Garden over 300 feet away. These girders destroyed other buildings such as the Deutsche Bank. All of the concrete floors were converted to extremely fine dust and little of the towers' structure remained except for some very tall sections of the core and perimeter structure at base.

In the case of buildings 4, 5, and 6 there centres were blown out leaving the rest of the structure intact - an outer shell, with office furniture remaining untouched. And some steel girders had 'rippled' ends. The whole plaza was like a bombed out city. On the following day not far away at Pier 92, Mayor Giuliani was to attend Exercise Tripod along with the Office of Emergency Management officials, police and firemen.

However FEMA had already turned up the day before. Another exercise involved an illusionary plane crash into a building and evacuation of personnel and a bio-terror exercise. This was cancelled immediately but Pier 92 became the OEM headquarters as WTC 7 had been evacuated early. Michael Hess head of OEM and Barry Jennings reportedly were trapped in WTC 7 and they said it was deserted apart from the firemen and the Secret Service stewards.

## Creative Artists

On 9/11, Lower Manhattan Cultural Council lost its home, performance venue, studio and exhibition spaces, and thirty years of archives. Michael Richards an artist-in-residence at the time fell to his death. The World Views residents were nearing the end of their session, and Michael had been working on the 91$^{st}$ floor of the North Tower. They said Michael had spent the night working in his 91$^{st}$ floor studio. However this was no proper studio, as it had no ceiling as you can see in the art students' photograph.

Michael was creating a sculpture inspired by the Tuskegee Airmen, which bore a strange parallel to the 9/11 tragedy. It is a sculpture of the artist in a gold suit with model airplanes sticking into his body. Another student was Monica Bravo making video recordings and who is now a celebrated artist. In 2005, LMCC received a $5 million grant from 'The September11th Fund' to support and sustain the arts community in Lower Manhattan.

Gelatin was an art team project using the 'B Thing'. It was ongoing from March 2000 by six of eighteen or more art students, included in several projects. They were filming and making drawings on the 91st floor outlining rough sketches and photographs of the place (10). They drew a cartoon of a falling body. One student is rigged in a safety harness ready for exit balcony would be camouflaged (11). They hired an attorney to oversee the project.

In the photographs of the 91st floor by Austrian art students the ceiling and carpets were gone, exposing the lagged pipes and the concrete floor. A pane of glass was removed on the 91st floor of the North Tower and a platform built to extend five feet outside (12). Here we see rope tethers tied to the bar truss, some black rope, some white, such that they would be tied from above to the daring model or figure. The photos of the balcony show a figure in the window, seemingly in a lectern in the narrow space between the exterior columns that appears to have been taken from the building opposite, or from the helicopter.

This project portrays a falling body and describes the inside of the building as a most depressing place. At this level they were able to sketch the basic structure according to the drawings. They have drawn exactly 240 columns including the four major corner columns and most of the core structure columns. The 9/11 ghost plane cut out by shaped charges occurred between 93$^{rd}$ and 99$^{th}$ floors in the North Tower.

## Observations

In the Naudet film inside the North Tower a mere handful of people came out of an elevator and a score more were seen exiting from the mezzanine floor, to another emergency exit. There were only a few reporters interviewing the supposed hundreds of evacuees from the buildings. Many witnesses reported seeing a plane either military or a Boeing but others said it was just an explosion.

Maintenance workers on the subway running underneath WTC stated that many of the kiosks were closed the morning of 9/11 and that had never happened before. There was a press photographer David Handschuh for New York Daily News in the street who got the explosion but he saw no plane (13). In the photograph we see the explosion and the structural material of the building falling away but no clear sign of aircraft debris, only the perimeter columns/panel sections. Only very recently did he say, on an internet video, that he did not see, nor hear a plane impact the building and this was its alleged point of entry, in the south face. He was apparently injured on 9/11 and was photographed on the floor of a shop and then being carried by firemen and a policeman.

In the North Tower that was hit first, Edna Cintron was the woman (14) identified as standing in the hole and waving on 9/11. The videos show there were no raging infernos prior to the Tower's collapse. The memorial photo of Edna had Exif/IPTC data embedded (15) on March 9, 2001, six months prior to 9/11.

Rosalee Grable the Web Fairy claimed: 'We know it is her because her family identified her by her hair, dress, and gutsy persistence. Edna is waving for a long time. She is waving when the fires are burning. She is still waving when the fires are out. For all of this time Edna is standing out on the edge, in a precarious position, when there are no flames or even smoke behind her or near her. But she stays and waves, instead of trying to escape to the safety of the building behind her, which is not on fire for most of the time.

One video from just before the Tower comes down, shows Edna still there but she is no longer waving. She is against a beam, and seems to be 'flapping' in the wind, like an effigy. She had moved higher up nearer to the smoke and fire. The Edna Cintron Hoax had one main objective, to convince us there were people trapped, waving for help, still present when the Tower came down.' (16).

# CHAPTER 11

## *Dark Forces: Total Destruction*

*Witchcraft is dark to the people because it is a rival power that the state will steal and blame and sacrifice for its own miscreant ends.*

A quote in the press states: 'Al Qaeda has sharply criticized Iran's ex-president, Mahmoud Ahmadinejad, over his suggestions that the U.S. government was behind the 9/11 attacks, dismissing his comments as ridiculous.' This was the same limited response from the CIA when La Figaro said bin Laden was being treated in the American hospital in Dubai in July 2001.

The pictures by FEMA and NIST contractors were obtained under the Freedom of Information act and show quite a lot of detail as to how the initial explosions cut the columns laterally, to effect a stepped pattern. It also shows how the trusses pulled the lower columns inwards, on collapse (17). The trusses were a lightweight structure but contained corrugated steel floors covered in four inches of lightweight concrete.

They were connected to the columns by welded angle iron with bolted joints. The viscoelastic dampers fixed the lower end sections of trusses to the perimeter columns. The trusses were connected between the core and perimeter columns to form a lattice structure. The core provided access to three levels by lifts and an express lift to the top in a tube structure containing separate tubes within it.

The unlikely theory of Dr Judy Wood in her book 'Where did the Towers Go' examines the evidence and proposes the use of 'Directed Free Energy' for the destruction of the towers and buildings. She says it is based on the work of Piggot and today Hutchinson. It uses directed energy, like microwaves, in a highly charged static field which cut or twist steel and can explode concrete into dust. However, most of the steel column structure and panels were flung beyond the towers.

The core of WTC 6 the Customs house was totally disintegrated leaving an outer shell of offices relatively untouched with floors and remaining structure intact. This was similar to the final collapse of the Pentagon leaving office walls and furniture and books intact, except WTC 6 left a massive crater (18). The Pentagon 'E' ring had sheared along the expansion joints from the use of explosives.

Evacuation and a Mystery Explosion

Christopher Bollyn an independent journalist said: 'Before the smoke had cleared from around the stricken South Tower, a mysterious explosion shot 550 feet into the air above the U.S. Customs House at WTC 6. This unexplained blast has never been reported in the mainstream media.'

It arose between the burning North Tower and WTC 7, just as the explosion occurred in the South Tower, at 9:03 a.m. The explosion at the eight-story WTC 6 was shown later on CNN. It was not broadcast live so there is doubt about the exact time it occurred. When Bollyn asked if the footage was taken at 9:04 a.m., the CNN archivist said, 'That's correct.' When asked if CNN could explain it he said, 'We can't figure it out.' WTC 6 housed the offices of some 760 employees of the Customs Service, a department of the U.S. Treasury. Other federal offices in the building included the Departments of Commerce, Agriculture, Labour, and the Bureau of Alcohol Tobacco & Firearms. [Christopher Bollyn - 10 July 2002].

A spokesman for an Export-Import Bank of the U.S., which had an office with four employees on the 6th floor of the Customs House, confirmed the time of the explosion and said the employees had been evacuated to another location. One private company, reportedly leased space in the building. Some 800 workers from WTC 6 were safely evacuated within twelve minutes of the first plane hitting the North Tower at 8:46 a.m., according to a news article - 'Knowing the Drill Saved Lives at New York's Customs House'.[Stephen Barr - Washington Post, 18 September 2001].

The Barr piece is the only known article published about WTC 6 at 9:04 a.m., the government-sponsored investigation was steered away from looking into what had actually happened. The Federal Emergency Management Agency funded an investigation by the American Society of Civil Engineers; however, investigators were blocked from the building by an order from the New York City's Dept. of Design and Construction.

Regarding the investigation of WTC 4, 5, and 6, FEMA's Building Performance Report says, 'WTC 5 was the only building open for observation. The findings and recommendations are assumed to be applicable to all three buildings.' A spokesman for

FEMA said that because the building was considered by the DDC to be very dangerous, there was no data collection from WTC 6.

One of the engineers who led the investigation said concerns about loose gold bullion and cash prevented investigators from entering WTC 4. The FEMA report says: The buildings 4, 5, and 6 responded as expected to the impact loadings (19). The report says, most of the central part of WTC 6 suffered collapse on all floors and adds, damage was consistent with the observed impact load. Just looking at the crater in WTC 6 shows this statement is false. The fallen panels from the South Tower are lying flat on the ground inside WTC6 but where did the core of the structure go - into the ground?

## What kind of Dark Forces?

Dr Wood shows the sub-basement car parks in WTC 4 and WTC 5 were unscathed so we can rule out bombs below ground here. However in WTC 6 all six sub car park levels were destroyed. It appeared there were at least two separate explosions. The first dust cloud billowing upwards to above WTC 7 was white and the second was sandy yellow. They left a massive crater with its core totally eradicated. This might suggest one of the explosions came from underground in the car parks of WTC 6 because of its sandy yellow colour.

Wood maintains that DFE was used on the WTC buildings eliciting criticism from both the nuke and thermite theorists accusing her of being a gatekeeper for the Government. Why so? She has gained access to scores of rare film footage; and her documentaries quash the absurd official accounts. The problem is how or from where could a 'free energy beam' have been directed or integrated within a 'powerful static field' over Manhattan. And the beam would have to be multi-directional at all levels with the source moving to focus on all target levels, or it must have had multiple sources.

There was a force three Hurricane Erin some 200 miles off the coast but it moved NE and although there was some distant thunder, NY was a perfectly clear sunny day. There is a top secret High-Frequency Active Auroral Research Program operated by the US Navy, based in remote Alaska. It can energise a charged atmosphere in its locality to some limited degree. The idea of a charged atmosphere to create a powerful static field for a directed energy weapon outside of a laboratory is still science fiction however. There are videos of disintegrating falling steel columns and a spire seemingly disintegrating into dust but this evidence is subjective as to cause. The spire was a single column of remnant core structure perhaps nearly 600 feet high that collapsed about twelve seconds after the building fell. It was shrouded in a dust cloud. The disintegration of the last of the core columns and the spire indicates a powerful explosive force associated with a gas/particle cloud enveloping the spire as it fell (20).

There is an argument here that supports the case for the use of barometric bombs, as they initiate by propagation of a particle cloud prior to ignition. One type projects a particle cloud of Al silicate/Pb azide infused with aqueous ammonium nitrate spray, in a two stage process as explained in Chapter 5. The cloud is highly charged and explodes by propagation from a high voltage dis-charge in the secondary stage. As the cloud travels some given distance before it explodes, it is able to propagate the explosive force in any given direction, with immense shattering power. Its blast velocity is up to 20 km per second.

An indication of barometric bombs is the variable cleavage patterns caused by the explosion. They destruct at random depending on the directional spread of the gas cloud as it is propelled on release. It consumes oxygen in the air as it travels and propagates the explosion till all the particle cloud is spent.

The spire was enveloped in a very energetic cloud travelling at about 40 mph upwards from its base on the ground some 600 feet. As it reached the spire - the structure was already collapsing. Finally it enshrouded the falling spire which seemed to disintegrate within the cloud. It might be that this was the last bomb at the base of the core, which was delayed. A barometric bomb cloud can be directional within 15 degrees and propagates as it travels such that any structure in its path is destroyed. The whole of the spire's remnant steel structure was under stress, or fractured, leading to final collapse, possibly initiated from the blast at the base of the structure.

Other extraneous effects were the destruction of scores of parked cars, trucks, fire engines, police cars and buses where the engines, bodies, tyres and door handles were either partially corroded, burnt out or missing (21). The windows were smashed and many roofs were not covered in falling debris. Why would police cars be abandoned or left so close to the towers? There were no reports of bodies being found in these vehicles. When the South Tower exploded there was a white cloud propagating from its base going upward but also another cloud travelling horizontally along-side the tower at street level.

FEMA acknowledges that roughly 90% of the Twin Towers' mass fell outside its footprints. The plaza was covered with steel pieces and assemblies. Some of the structural steel was thrown as far away as the Winter Garden. Many of the core box columns found in the WTC rubble had concave sides. They were broken straight across at the joints whilst other columns at the base of the towers were cut at angles. Often, one side of the broken column zones were deeply oxidized and torn away. In demolition, line charges are placed against the steel at a nominal 45 degree angle to cut the steel and allow the upper section to slip apart, under gravity, to aid separation.

Explosions severed the core columns, as explained by Gordon Ross a Scottish Mechanical Engineer; he offers an explosive hypothesis that demonstrates a mechanism with results resembling observations in the WTC rubble.

Ross described how the severed sections are concave on opposite faces caused by explosive force, ripping across the steel or its joints horizontally, due to concussion explosives. These were likely placed on every third floor in the structure, mainly at their joints. The core structure was attacked first as we see the North Tower mast begin to collapse into its core. Not all of the core columns were severed successfully but all of the strongest columns closer in to the elevator shafts were severed by the charges.

There were several phases of attack. Prior to collapse the four corners of the perimeter columns were cut using incendiary charges at two or three major sections of the towers possibly. These were the major seats of failure in the perimeter structure. This was observed on film as white flashes at the corners, as the collapse progressed. At one corner section on the 81st floor, a major seat of failure, molten metal was seen pouring down from the structure well prior to collapse (22).

The remaining perimeter columns may have suffered catastrophic collapse breaking away from the building as the joints failed, if not aided by more explosive charges or from the blast effects from the core explosions. Some of the panels came away under high force landing dozens of yards from the building. Some connected panels of perimeter columns in the debris were massive - up to twenty columns, others just several columns per panel.

The lateral joints were welded angle iron containing bolts to connect the steel trusses to the columns. The vertical column sections were connected together by the much stronger spandrel plates. Individual columns were connected by four plate bolts or alternatively by twelve column bolts with two columns to every spandrel plate.

Whole sections of the perimeter columns were seen to have fallen away. The joints may have failed between the trusses and the perimeter structure due to the massive force of the exploding and collapsing core. The core columns were possibly severed on every third floor as seen in the rapid downward progression of white smoke or dust squibs exiting the perimeter, according to Ross. Several of the core columns survived till last to collapse. An example is that of a section of core structure left a towering spire that finally collapsed at the last.

There was no public evidence of body parts discovered in the total debris. This contradicts all known experience of building collapses whether from fire, earthquake or explosions. The buildings must have been evacuated for the controlled demolition to be sanctioned.

## High Order Damage

The destruction of the Twin Towers matches fully the characteristics of high-order damage as they are listed in the NFPA 921 Guide for Fire and Explosion Investigations. All three WTC skyscrapers were completely destroyed; their structural units and perimeter walls were shattered. Heavy pieces from the Twin Towers were thrown horizontally at seventy mph over large distances, and most of the concrete floors were finely pulverized. The theory of high-order damage is from evidence that explosions with a high rate of pressure rise occurred. The use of high explosives explains all the evidence that matches the characteristics of high-order damage.

The explosive evidence is held by over one hundred accounts of firefighters, many of whom reported sounds of explosions and patterned flashes of light, with many inferring the destruction as being caused by secondary devices. Substantial quantities of previously molten iron spheres, up to one hundred and fifty times the background level of iron in dust from other buildings in the area, were found and documented by the US Geological Survey and the RJ Lee Group. RJ Lee found the microspheres in amounts up to 6% inside the skyscraper across the street from WTC 2. Other scientists estimate a total of 10-100 tons of microspheres altogether throughout Lower Manhattan. These spheres were so abundant that RJ Lee used them as a signature component of the WTC Dust. RJ Lee notes that the microspheres were created during the event and not by welding operations during the clean-up of Ground Zero. Office fires and jet fuel fires could not possibly have produced them.

The chemical signature of the examined spheres matched the chemical signature of spheroids produced by thermite and by red/grey Nano - thermite composite chips found in the WTC dust, indicating that thermitic reactions took place as part of the towers' demolition. Molten metal was observed pouring from WTC 2 several minutes before its final destruction. FEMA's Building Performance Assessment Team report documents molten iron invading the grain boundaries of the WTC structural steel. A NY Times article called this the deepest mystery of the investigation. Thermitic materials produce molten iron at 4,500° F temperatures. They can easily cut through steel and create the ubiquitous iron spheroids. An international research team found Nano - engineered thermite in each of the four samples of dust examined as part of a peer-reviewed study.

Nano - thermite was developed in US national laboratories in the late 1990s as an energetic composite material, meaning it could serve as a pyrotechnic substance to ignite other energetic materials, such as a rocket fuel, or as an explosive unto itself with advantages over conventional high explosives. The red/grey chips show evidence of the explosive/ incendiary hypothesis. The American Society of Safety Engineers reported that 'the debris pile at Ground Zero was always tremendously hot. Thermal measurements taken by helicopter each day showed underground temperatures ranging from 400°F to more than 2,800°F.'

The original theory of a 'pancake' collapse due to simultaneous failure of thousands of bolts from a gravity driven collapse was found not to be tenable. Insurance companies stated the clause covered no pay out for this. Indeed Dr Eager of MIT backed this dubious theory by stating that the steel structure had failed due to residual heat from the fuel explosion causing bolts and welds to fail in the trusses. For this to happen the steel structure would have to be heated well beyond its yield point into an elastic and then into a plasticed state. And then for all of the joints to simultaneously fail at a rate of 400 joints (or connections) per second. Only explosions could break the connections which are designed to fail at least 1.2 times above the load failure of the steel structure itself.

NIST re- examined the cause and stated it was critical column failure causing collapse due to intense heat deformation of the steel trusses, initiating collapse from just below the top of the upper section of the towers. This, however impossible a cause, would give an assymetric collapse and would topple only the top section; as we saw the South Tower topple before it was corrected by many more explosions. The NIST theory implies gravity collapse through the line of maximum resistance down the rest of the tower itself. In reality we see explosions occurring from the top down. However no explanation was given for the core's collapse since this would have remained standing according to both of these theories. Such a plane, or its engines, could not possibly penetrate to the core structure through the tight web of boxed steel columns. In one video the squibs were seen to be coming out of the perimeter in direct line with one side of the central core and rapidly progressing downward at about every third floor.

As seen in the photographs the steel was severed through, as if cut or broken (23). The melting point of steel is over 2500 degrees F but the steel appears to have undergone terrific torque pressures to bend and break as explained by Gordon Ross (24). In the North Tower the mast began sinking into the structure before total collapse. The towers started collapsing from the top section e.g. in the South Tower a 30 storey block toppled over at 23 degrees before it was disintegrated in a few seconds. According to the law of conservation of angular momentum, a freely turning body will keep turning unless opposed by another force. This force was explosive destruction. This proceeded at consecutive floors as estimated by observation of the procession of puffs or squibs down the towers, as seen in the videos.

One girder, of 30 tons, twice the weight of a Boeing, was flung into the World Financial Centre 400 feet away in Vesey Street. A massive girder buried itself into the empty Deustche Bank which was finally demolished years later. Except for some artefacts (25) there was little evidence of office furniture, telephones, and computers except for paper sheets - hundreds of them. They were coming out of the building well before collapse.

## Disintegration and Tainted Evidence

The absence of contents would be normal in controlled demolition since all buildings are gutted of floors, walls and fabrics to ensure a symmetric collapse. However five years later 700 tiny fragments of human bones were found on top of the Deutsche Bank prior to its demolition, allegedly. No fuel explosion could totally disintegrate bones embedded and cushioned in the human body. It would not account for the total absence of thousands of body parts either. The lightweight concrete floors were pulverised. The explosives were likely set in the steel structure, at the joints, in which the floors were laid onto the trusses. So the detonation wave likely passed directly through the rigid floors.

The bone splinters were 'found' years later when little or no evidence of dead bodies were found at the time. It would take a mincing machine to crush bones into tiny slithers. The paper sheets survived intact because they were not embedded in the structure and were simply propelled into the air before the collapse.

A certain NY Medical Officer was Director of Forensic Biology in identifying particulate body parts from the Towers and 'identified' many victims of the families. This man was a defendant in a recent New Jersey suit whereby the plaintiff accused him of fraud. The plaintiff's appeal from the trial court's September 12, 2012 order was dismissed in his complaint against defendant, whom he retained as a testimonial expert in a post-conviction relief hearing.

Plaintiff alleged that he hired the medical officer as an expert in DNA evidence, because he said to plaintiff that he would give specific testimony before the court.

In particular, he asserted that the defendant had said that certain forensic reports that the State submitted in plaintiff's trial were 'improperly prepared and contained tainted evidence.' Defendant falsely assured the plaintiff he would testify that the State DNA report contained tainted evidence. The Plaintiff lost his case and may have to serve 18 years for allegedly raping his girlfriend based on tainted evidence despite the testimony of the medical officer.

## Demolition and Salvage

The 9/11 truth movement and associates including Steven Jones, David Ray Griffin, Richard Gage, Kevin Ryan, Barry Zwigger et al have attested, or generally accepted, the three main towers were brought down by controlled demolition, whether or not in conjunction with a Boeing or some other kind of air borne attack. Experts in controlled demolition have vouched and explained how the techniques are carried out. The South Tower top section separated and started to topple first then explosive devices began to destroy it as it toppled. In the North Tower the mast started to sink into the mass of its core centre indicating that the core collapsed first.

The core base columns and major tower perimeter corner sections were likely cut prior to collapse using a combination of cutting processes. This included the placement of concussion charges or shaped charges and possibly in conjunction with the use of incendiary's, thermite or Nano - thermite. The latter would explain the molten steel which flowed and continued to propagate under ground zero for weeks. In addition analysis of dust samples by various laboratories proved the presence of thermite, including chemical analysis by international bodies and universities.

A great number of powerful high order explosive devices were used to disintegrate the floors converting them to dust. The blasting power was sufficient to propel much of the steel structure well beyond the building and shatter windows hundreds of feet away. Dust squibs from the gravity collapse theory could not possibly generate the power blasts required to break distant windows that was more likely caused by high explosive shock waves and falling debris. It is unproven that many hundreds of people were killed or severely injured in this operation since no certain public evidence of human bones or body parts were found in the rubble. Senator John Kerry stated that WTC 7 was brought down in a controlled fashion but refused to answer any further questions on the subject. It is not easily possible to bring tall buildings down in near symmetry without many days of preparation and ensuring removal and stripping of contents but this was not a normal demolition since most of the structure was exploded beyond the building.

Most of the steel was immediately loaded onto trucks and exported to the Far East in the business as usual removal of evidence. A lot of it was stored on a New Jersey scrap metal site prior to selling it off to foreign scrap merchants. It was planned to have no investigation at all. The 'Jersey Girls' campaign finally got the Administration to create the 9/11 Commission headed and chaired by Thomas H Kean and Executive Director Philip Zelikow and vice-chaired by Lee Hamilton, after 440 days. Initially Henry Kissinger had been chosen to head the Commission but quickly resigned after a discussion with the Jersey girls.

## Gold and Silver Haul

On November 01, 2001 the Times Online reported in New York: 'Recovery workers at Ground Zero have discovered hundreds of gold ingots, part of a billion dollar cache which was lost when the twin towers fell. Workers clearing rubble in a service tunnel underneath one of the collapsed World Trade Centre buildings were soon surrounded by armed FBI and secret service personnel. The collapsed buildings contained a number of vaults and strong rooms. They kept 3,800 gold bars, worth more than $100 million, in the basement vaults. It held gold ounces there with a value of about $220 million. It also held more than 102 million ounces of silver, worth $430 million.

The banks which kept gold in the vault, reported $200 million of gold lost in the wreckage. Recovery workers reached a service tunnel and discovered a ten-wheel lorry and a number of cars which had been crushed by falling steel. A ramp was built to gain access to the tunnel and a small bulldozer was used to break through a wall. A team of police and firefighters arrived to put the gold into an armoured bullion lorry.' In 1993 when the World Trade Centre was bombed by terrorists, more than $1 billion in gold was being kept in the basement vaults. The vaults withstood the blast. At first police believed the terrorist attack was an attempted gold robbery. Since then the amount of gold kept under the World Trade Centre was kept secret.

# CHAPTER 12

## Attack on the Pentagon

### Look, up in the sky! It's a Bird! It's a Plane! No, it's Superman.

The Transport Secretary Norman Mineta gave his testimony to the 9/11 Commission about what he witnessed in the Presidential Emergency Operating Centre. He was with Vice President Cheney as AA flight 77 headed towards the Pentagon. This account was not included in the 9/11 Commission Report. In the soliloquy testified by Mineta, Cheney refers to orders concerning the plane approaching the Pentagon:

"There was a young man who had come in and said to the vice president, the plane is 50 miles out. The plane is 30 miles out. And when it got down to, the plane is 10 miles out, the young man also said to the vice president, 'Do the orders still stand?' And the vice president turned and whipped his neck around and said, 'Of course the orders still stand. Have you heard anything to the contrary?' Well, at the time I didn't know what all that meant." Commissioner Lee Hamilton queried if the order was to shoot down the plane, to which Mineta replied that he did not know that specifically.

Mineta's testimony differs significantly from his earlier account given in the January 22, 2002 edition of The Washington Post, as reported by Bob Woodward and Dan Balz. Their account says that at 9:26 a.m. the Vice President was in the bunker. He was in touch with Mr. Bush and Norman was summoned by the White House to the bunker. Mineta took an open line to the Federal Aviation Administration operations centre, monitoring Flight 77 as it headed toward Washington, with radar tracks coming in every seven seconds. Reports came in that the plane was fifty miles out, thirty miles out, ten miles out - until word reached the bunker that there had been an explosion at the Pentagon. Mineta shouted into the phone to Monte Belger at the FAA: 'Monte, bring all the planes down.'

It was an unprecedented order - there were 4,546 airplanes in the air at the time. Belger, the FAA's acting deputy administrator, amended Mineta's directive to take into account the authority vested in airline pilots. 'We're bringing them down per pilot discretion,' Belger told the secretary. '[Expletive] pilot discretion,' Mineta yelled back. 'Get those [expletive] planes down.' Sitting at the other end of the table, Cheney snapped his head up, looked squarely at Mineta and nodded in agreement.

This same article reports that the conversation between Cheney and the aide occurred at about 9:55 a.m., thirty minutes later than the time Mineta cited (9:26) during his testimony to the 9/11 Commission. The time of 9.26 given to the Commission would be the more accurate time frame of the white jet approaching fifty miles away at say 450 mph to hit at 9.32. However, Cheney had said that he was not in the bunker until after 9.50, according to the 9/11 Commission. It might appear that Cheney's story was changed so that he gave the order to shoot the plane down at 9.55, instead of letting it be. An explanation was that the plane had turned away and then came back for a second attempt. This however contradicts with Mineta's later statement to the Commission and also conflicts with the official time of 9.37 for the strike.

## Distraction

An E-4B was flying over Washington just before 10 a.m. during the attack on the Pentagon (26). The Boeing E-4 Advanced Airborne Command Post, with the project name Nightwatch, is an aircraft operated by the United States Air Force. To create the E-4 series, four Boeing 747-200B airframes were specially modified to serve as a survivable mobile command post for the National Command Authority, namely the President of the United States, the Secretary of Defence, and successors. The four E-4Bs are operated by the 1st Airborne Command and Control Squadron of the 55th Wing located at Offutt Air Force Base, near Omaha, Nebraska. An E-4B is denoted a National Airborne Operations Centre when in action. The large hump on the dorsal surface contains the aircraft's SHF satellite antenna. Witnesses say that this was the Boeing aircraft seen over Washington and the White House - over a restricted zone and assumed to be Flight 77.

## Robot Attack

The military attack on the Pentagon is certain because of the evidence that some kind of missile or craft was observed manoeuvring at high speed and caused an explosion with extensive debris. A non-military or alien craft would likely be shot down by the defence batteries unless de-commissioned. Evidence came from air traffic controllers, witnesses, photographs of the debris and two fake video clips eventually released by the FBI from 85 they withheld; and the sworn negative evidence of Officer Maguire saying the remaining tapes showed nothing of a Boeing (44).

The portion of the Pentagon targeted was mostly unoccupied due to a renovation program. The attack plane executed an extreme spiral dive manoeuvre to hit that portion of the building rather than the part housing high-level officials. The nature of the approach and attack dive itself was consistent with something other than a 757 as the air traffic controller Danielle O'Brien stated:

'We started moving the planes as quickly as we could,' she told ABC News. 'Then we noticed the aircraft. It was an unidentified plane to the southwest of Dulles, moving at a very high rate of speed. I had literally a blip on my radar screen and nothing more.' O'Brien got the alien blip to the attention of her colleague, Tom Howell. He said to ABC News:

'We've got a target headed right for the White House.' It was heading toward towards protected air space P56 that shields the White House and the Capitol. 'The speed, the manoeuvrability, the way that he turned, we all thought in the radar room, all of us experienced air traffic controllers, that it was a military plane,' O'Brien said.

As you will see below the Pentagon was attacked by a self-propelled military aircraft, or a UAV, which exploded at the Pentagon wall at 9.32 a.m.; its left wing touched the ground prior to disintegration, coincidentally as a military helicopter took off from the helipad just three seconds before the plane crashed. The helicopter had just landed 5 minutes earlier at 9.27 a.m. having been seen by an ex naval pilot, from his hotel. This sighting was confirmed by Reagan National airport showing it was a Marine Call helicopter according to Barbara Honegger. According to a naval historian this helicopter was sent by the White House - probably by Dick Cheney who was in charge in the bunker, to destroy the plane.

## Double Trouble

The following account of what happened at the Pentagon is given by Barbara Honegger (Researcher at the US Navy Post Graduate College) for her new book 'Behind the Smoke Curtain'. Her research is detailed enough to give evidence that cannot easily be refuted as it is based on genuine official records, timings and crucial evidence from firemen, junior and senior defence staff and some rare original photographs. Her main theme is based on a white plane attack at 9.32 a.m. including explosions with associated damage points in both Wedge1 and 2 on the west side. She gives a chronological order of events:

9.30 Wedge 2: Outer 'E' Ring damaged. Evidence April Gallop's wrist watch stopped and her office is heavily damaged.

9.31 Wedge 2: 'D' Ring. Navy clock is stopped.

9.32 Wedge 2: Outside 'E' ring wall. White plane explodes in flight near building just after a Huey helicopter arrived.

9.34 Wedge1: A nearby diesel trailer is set on fire causing a rising black billowing smoke screen.

9.43 Wedge1: Rings E, D and C damaged by a massive explosion, and an orange ball of fire, centred on the alleged strike point, at column 14 of the outer E ring. Four columns are severed plus four columns are damaged. It is recorded on seismic data by the USGS station 38 miles from the Pentagon.

9.48 Wedge1: Large explosion recorded by Secret Service Log.

10.10 Wedge1: The final collapse occurs at the alleged strike point. A second massive explosion is recorded on seismic data by the USGS station (34), (41).

At 9.30 there was an internal explosion near the comp-controller's department according to April Gallop's wrist watch. The computers were hot and smoking and the office walls damaged. Her baby was covered in dust and she got to it and then found a ground floor exit window to climb out. There was a fire engine already parked there near the helipad. Her colleagues also got out without injury.

At 9.32 a white plane travelling at some speed, exploded in front of Wedge 2 near to the helipad and caused fires on the lawn and the trees close to the building. Its left wing tip had just grazed the ground. This was witnessed by three fire-fighters, two of whom had just moved the fire truck out of the fire-house and backed it against the Pentagon wall. They were expecting a visit from President Bush after 12 o'clock.

One fireman saw the white craft approaching and dived beneath the vehicle for safety before the left wing touched ground. A despatcher, Sean Boger, was in the tower of the firehouse and he saw the plane make an approach and explode near the helipad. His colleague had just departed the tower.

A military helicopter (H53 Huey) had already arrived at 9.27. It had been zig- zagging about waiting to land according to an ex- navy pilot, as seen from his hotel. It arrived just minutes before the white plane exploded within yards of the airborne helicopter. The timings of both craft were recorded at Reagan National Airport. The plane was a jet engine craft that had exploded causing the debris field (27). It exploded near the helipad about 150 feet north of the alleged strike point and caused barely any damage to the non-reinforced Wedge 2; it left soot deposits and two burnt trees at the wall and burnt grass (31).

One witness said we could not see the plane. The only thing that we saw was a piece of the front skin with the "C" from American Airlines by the little heliport control tower (28). (It was probably the 'n' piece as seen in the photograph). There was a fire truck there that was burnt on one side, and a car, and a tree, all burnt. But, still, you could not see the plane.

Another witness saw a silver commuter jet fly past the window of his 14th floor apartment in Pentagon City. The plane was about 150 yards away, approaching from the west about twenty feet off the ground. It sounded like the high-pitched squeal of a fighter over Arlington cemetery so low that he thought it was going to land on I-395. The plane, which appeared to hold about eight to twelve people, headed straight for the Pentagon. Then, he said, he saw the Pentagon envelop the plane and bright orange flames shoot out the back of the building.

The debris was scattered some distance and a lady witness saw the plane coming in very low to the north side of the Citgo Garage and over the Columbia Pike Rd. She was located on Route 27 stuck in traffic and very close to the Pentagon. She recovered a piece of it that had landed on her car. It was of a white outer shell and inner section of a fibre like material. Soon dozens of Pentagon staff and FBI combed the area in a line picking up debris from the lawn, south to north. The FBI took away the video images from the Citgo garage, the highway and nearby hotels in addition to the Pentagon's cameras - eighty six in total. Also they carried away a box framed object covered in standard blue nylon tarpaulin (46).

A member of the Fort Myer Fire Department arrived a few minutes after the attack. Yet, expecting to see pieces of the wings or fuselage, he instead reportedly sees 'millions' of tiny pieces of debris spread everywhere.

An officer of the Metropolitan Washington Airports Authority Fire Department also arrives within minutes of the crash. He recalled: 'The near total disintegration of the plane had left only a multitude of bits scattered outside the building.'

A helicopter pilot with the US Park Police arrives over the Pentagon in his helicopter shortly after 9:37 a.m. 'It was a relatively small hole in the side of the building (42). I'm going. This couldn't possibly have been a 757. I just can't emphasize enough, the initial damage, looking at it; it just didn't look like a 757 hit that building.' [US Naval Historical Centre, 11/20/2001].

Another Park Police helicopter pilot landed his helicopter near the crash site shortly after the attack. He said: 'When I landed on the scene, there was actually a particular slit into the side of the Pentagon, which is hard to believe that an aircraft made it, but it's that small of a slit. I could not see any aviation parts. I couldn't see an engine or a wing. There was just rubble, pieces, small pieces.' [US naval historical centre, 11/19/2001].

Another witness said: '... when I looked at the site, my brain could not resolve the fact that it was a plane because it only seemed like a small hole in the building. No tail. No wings. No nothing.' [Scripps Howard News Service, 8/1/2002].

General Hugh Shelton Chairman of the Joint Chiefs of Staff quoted 'there was a distinct smell of cordite in the building' when he arrived. He was heading for Hungary via London for a NATO meeting, on his plane the Speckled Trout. It returned 'over Manhattan' before noon after it had been delayed over Greenland waiting for permission to land. They landed at Andrews AF base at 4.40 pm and drove to his office at Pentagon. He saw the devastation over Manhattan that caused his delay in getting back to Meyers at 5.40 pm at the National Military Command Centre and resuming command.

## Props

There is an identifiable piece of the fuselage of the alleged 757 in the photo by Mark Faram (28). It does appear to be the genuine starboard side of a 757. As you can see it lies some distance from the building. A witness of the plane said: 'I looked out my window and I saw this plane, this jet, an American Airlines jet, coming. And I thought, this doesn't add up, it's really low. I mean it was like a cruise missile with wings.' Many features of the crash site show photographs that support evidence against the crash of a 757.

Damaged columns remain standing where steel parts of the plane, such as the engine, would have left remnants. Pristine limestone and unbroken windows are visible in areas where the outer wings and vertical tail section of a 757 would have hit. There were obstacles in the plane's alleged flight path (45), such as cable spools and five lamp posts allegedly knocked down. The first post was lying on the freeway alongside a stationary taxi cab.

The first lamp post 'was hit' on the interstate highway and went through the windscreen of a Taxi cab driver, located on Interstate I 395 bridge. This pole was over thirty five feet long weighing 247 lbs. He said he removed the pole with the help of another driver. There was no sign of damage on the hood of the car just a smashed windscreen. His wife worked for the FBI and he later quoted on film that the 'facts' were just too big to argue with.

In addition the official story says the Boeing struck a generator (or diesel trailer) which is the cause of the black smoke to the right of the first major explosion, as seen in the photograph. So that would mean the wings struck five streetlamps and the generator, which is impossible. Any plane would crash land if it grazed just one lamp post with its wing, as does occur infrequently. The wings of a Boeing have reserve aviation fuel tanks.

## Ground Level Aerobatics

The destruction of the ground floor columns either partial or complete was drastic, causing the concrete to disintegrate to slag leaving steel re-bar skeletons. Of eight outer columns in Wedge 1, ten feet apart, only four were severed completely. These columns were centred on column fourteen in the zone of the alleged strike point on the ground floor where 95% of the damage occurred. See the official diagram showing the 'path of the craft' through rings E, D and C. The Punch Out is at the A-E drive showing a debris field and the rescue or retrieval point here (37), (38), (40).

There was a white smoke trail shown in the videos released by the FBI. There was not one eyewitness reporting the trail of white smoke lingering above the lawn. The videos are suspect because of the date 9/12 (43). A Boeing aircraft did not fly low across the lawn and impact the Pentagon. That would be totally impossible with the Citizens report saying the actual aircraft flew over the Naval Annex and north of the Citgo garage. To have caused the ground floor damage in the narrow slit, no more than seventy feet wide and twelve feet high, would have meant the engines ploughing into the ground but the grass lawn was pristine near the alleged strike point at Wedge1.

## Damage Control

The government commissioned Pentagon Building Performance Report acknowledges that there was no damage to the building from either the wings or the tail of the plane, which would have reached up to the fourth floor of the building which is seventy feet high. The Pentagon report feebly suggested that the wings and tail folded up and followed the nose and fuselage of the plane into the building. The only video that the FBI released of the explosion appears to be missing some frames.

At Wedge 2 trees and cars were burnt here, where the white jet crashed. The white plane exploded near the trees at 9.32 am. Then a major controlled explosion blew out a seventy foot slit on ground floor and a segment of 1$^{st}$ floor at 9.43 a.m. according to Honegger. The official time however was 9.37 a.m. The final explosion occurred at Wedge 1 on the right at 10.10 a.m. that caused the E ring to collapse along an expansion (or construction) joint.

Other government officials, or FBI agents, not rescue workers were photographed, moving evidence around within minutes after the Pentagon crash (32). FBI agents quickly confiscated a videotape from the Citgo gas station, Sheraton Hotel and film from the

Virginia Transportation Department freeway overpass camera. Air traffic controllers from the Washington DC sector, originally said the incoming plane was a military jet, according to the first press reports. The three aircraft parts found, were similar to the outdated but serviceable Douglas A3 Sky warrior military attack jet.

At the front hall of the E ring lying against the wall was a broken piece of the big wing of the craft. No reporters or independent experts were allowed to inspect any of the recovered aircraft parts. The broken wing section (35) in the photograph looks to be from an A3 Sky Warrior variant because they have similar geometry corresponding to the hinged flaps of an A3 Sky Warrior. This is seen by comparing the two broken hinged flap wing sections (47) being lifted by a crane, with the A3 Sky Warrior wing flaps on the aircraft carrier (48).[Courtesy of Geoff Deryk].

## Walking Wounded

In the army section a senior officer Lt. Col. Brian Birdwell survived because he happened to visit the toilet. He related his story many months later and has several online videos. He had a neat black head band and surgical gloves and no visible sign of burns whilst he described 60% coverage of severe burns to his body. Only his big feet were fully spared from the blaze. In telling his story he described three levels of pain and how a broken water pipe sprayed water onto his body protecting him from the burning inferno. He believed the Lord saved him for a good purpose. Indeed although he was 'consumed by the flames' the water spray saved him. His shirt and vest was 'burnt off his body' and even his security badge was burnt so he could not escape the building, till rescued. The hell he went through in recovery whilst vouching revenge – he remembered how Jesus died on the cross for all of us and then his anger subsided. He later became a Texas Senator - after the President had visited him in hospital to salute him. To give the kind gentleman credit he did confirm the E ring finally collapsed -straight along its construction joint (36).

In the army section April Gallop survived the acceptable collateral damage, in Wedge 2 offices, along with her colleagues. Later, April took her case for blame against Dick Cheney, Don Rumsfeld and General Meyers to the federal district court but it was thrown out by Judge Denny Chin in 2009. She took it to Second Circuit Court in 2011 and it was overruled by three judges in New Haven, Connecticut.

The Pentagon attack was planned to be a fail safe operation because all of the offices in the Wedge 1 including the Navy Wing were bomb proofed and probably empty. April was in the army section located in the outer E ring of Wedge 2 and exited from a window behind a parked fire truck near the heliport. She said there was no sign of plane wreckage inside the building. There were no serious injuries reported here and all her colleagues got out safely she said.

In the navy section eleven officers were allegedly inside a bomb proof room in ring C. Only one had survived. He reported a major explosion occurred at 9.43 a.m. A series of explosions had occurred according to another officer in the first floor D ring of the Naval Command Centre (30), (39).

The evidence of serious injury or death is not visible in all the photographs released by the FBI and the media. However the listed deaths for the Pentagon give around 189 including 64 in the plane including 'two Raytheon executives'. That Raytheon should lose three more people on different flights on 9/11 is more than questionable. The final official Pentagon report stated there were remains of five bodies in the C ring rubble. This rubble including its 'unidentifiable' remains were re-incinerated and dumped in the Dover, Delaware landfill.

## Private Investigations

According to Tom Flocco an independent investigative journalist - 'Five of Raytheon's staff tied to the Global Hawk Remote-Controlled UAV Aircraft Systems allegedly died without a Grand Jury probing their members' electronic messages, or phone records, meeting calendars, visits or calls. Two civilian defence contractors to the US Air Force were working at commercial corporate facilities in the months before 9/11. They completely refitted and modified A-3 Sky Warrior aircraft at a small civilian airport in Colorado.'

Karl Schwarz a presidential candidate said: 'the Air Force brought in separate teams to do top-secret military work unrelated to commercial aviation at this airport.' Schwarz is the CEO of a company which designs remote control/UAVs for the U.S. Army and had a $392 million dollar Defence Department order for thirty two UAVs cancelled. He is a former Republican from Arkansas now living in Georgia and was running as an Independent to clean up government corruption and crime.

Air-traffic controllers from the Washington, DC sector originally said the incoming plane was a military jet. Schwarz said the time-line of secret refitting prior to the attacks and recovered parts coincides with the A3 attack jet found at the Pentagon. 'The Air Force has four to six A3s in current operation,' said Schwarz. The plane used at the Pentagon may have been brought in from Arizona from an Air Force Base which has numerous old planes taken out of service and stored there in the desert. The use of an out of service plane would disguise the source of the actual jet.

Schwarz also said 'one crew came in to fit the jet for remote-UAV systems, another crew put in the fire control systems and another installed the new jet engines, another the AGMs. The diffuser case recovered after the impact is a component from the types of dual-chamber turbo jets represented by the Allison J33, J71 Pratt & Whitney Jade 57 and JT8D. (49). The difference is between the dual-chamber turbojets and the newer high bypass jet fan designs found on the 757 and 767 jets. The Boeing diffuser case has triangular bezels around the openings.'(50). The A3 diffuser case has oval bezels. (51).

Another component found at the Pentagon was a wheel hub, a type made by an aerospace division. Schwarz said: 'They also made the wheels for the 757 but a simple proportional check of width versus diameter show that the photo is not a wheel hub from a 757, which has a much larger radius than width. The Pentagon wheel hub is the type used for aircraft carrier-based or smaller military planes.' (52).

In April 2005, an American writer Chevalier Désireé in France revealed that Russia watched on their satellite as the alleged A3 Sky warrior left a carrier and impacted the Pentagon. It would appear that Russian satellites photographed a ship-launched craft that crashed at the Pentagon that has been withheld from the public. The localities of two ships were the aircraft carrier George Washington off Long Island and the John F Kennedy off Virginia.

# CHAPTER 13

## The Shanksville Legend

*Fool me once shame on you.
Fool me twice shame on me.*

Flight 93 was destined to go down in folk lore. The famous 'Let's Roll' cry from Tod Beamer echoed across the nation. But we need to discover certain facts that will reveal proof that Flight 93 landed safely at John Hopkins that day; thanks to the Pilots for Truth.

From the start the United 93 crash revealed no evidence of body or plane debris - just a smoking hole in the ground. This hole was an abandoned mine shaft or sink hole that showed up on US Geological Survey charts beforehand. The coroner stated there was no victims but later returned to find DNA evidence and 'several arms and legs'. It is odd that he is forced to go back and prove that the bodies have disintegrated or were converted to particulate matter just like the bodies and material parts converted to dust at the Towers and the Pentagon. Even the Mayor saw no evidence of bodies or major plane wreckage.

The Bureau of Transportation Statistics confirms that both United Flights 93 and 175 were airborne on 9/11. The FAA records show the planes were not deregulated until Sept 2005. There is no available data to show the American Airlines flight schedules 11 and 77 were airborne, except from the media. BTS records however, show they were not scheduled to fly that day. John Lear, son of the inventor of the Lear Jet and Gerard Holmgren after exhaustive research, amongst other reputable sources, stated that there were no commercial passenger jets involved in any of the four 9/11 incidents.

On 9/11 at 9.03 (EDT), Flight UA 175 responded automatically using its Aircraft Address Reporting System - ACARS. This reply confirmed it was flying within a hundred mile vicinity of Middleton, Harrisburg flying west and parallel to Pittsburgh by 9.20 a.m. according to the despatchers: Ed Ballinger, Gerry Tsen and Ad Rogers' recorded messages - obtained by Pilots for Truth.

A Delta 1989 landed at Hopkins Airport, Cleveland and the passengers eventually disembarked and were escorted to the NASA Flight Research building there. The plane had landed at 9.47 a.m. (13.47 GMT) according to the National Commission on Terrorism but Delta Airlines said it landed at 10.10 a.m. It is suggested that UA 175 had changed its transponder signal and authorisation protocol to Delta 1989 based on messages routed to United 175, N612U. The sixty nine passengers were kept on this plane for over two hours and witnessed another plane landing. At 11.00 a.m. (15.00 GMT) Mayor White informed everyone that a 767 Boeing made an emergency landing due to a bomb threat but no bomb was found. It was flying from Boston to Los Angeles. All people in the airport were ordered to evacuate on foot immediately under security orders.

## The Location of Flight UA 93

The second plane was UA 93 which flew over Champaign, IL at 10.10 a.m. (14.10 GMT) according to its ACARS message and it then landed at John Hopkins, Cleveland at 10.45 a.m. (14.45 GMT). The two Boeings were flights UA 175 and 93 according to all known data. At 10.10 a.m. the FAA had ordered all commercial planes to land. At 11.43 a.m. United confirmed that UA 93 had landed at Hopkins.

More information has surfaced which conclusively demonstrates the aircraft reportedly used on 9/11, were airborne well after their alleged crashes. ACARS determines if a message is received by the aircraft, along with how ground stations are selected through Flight Tracking Protocol.

The data places United 93 N591UA, in the vicinity of Champaign, IL, 500+ miles away from the alleged crash site in Shanksville, PA. This information was further corroborated by a senior member of the airline staff. He gave an interview to the FBI at United Headquarters and reviewed a list of ACARS messages explaining the contents and which messages were received or rejected. The messages provided below conflicts with the 9/11 Commission findings. Two messages were routed through the Fort Wayne, Indiana remote ground stations (FWA), followed by two more messages which were routed through Champaign, IL (CMI).

The remote ground station used to route the message to the aircraft (FWA or CMI), the time and date in which the message is sent (e.g. 111351, meaning the 11th of Sept, at 13.51 GMT), the flight number (UA93), and the tail number of the airplane in which the message is intended (N591UA). The underlined date and time is when the message was received by the airplane. Although the first two appear to be identical, the message number denotes that they are in fact two separate messages. The 4 messages to UA93 were as follows:

First message:

DDLXCXA CHIAK CHI68R

CHIAKUA 111351/ED

AGM

AN N591UA/GL FWA

UA93 EWRSFO

MESSAGE FROM CHIDD -

LAND ASP AT NEAREST -- NEAREST AIRPORT. ASP .ASP ON GROND.ANYWERE.

CHIDD ED BALLINGER

09111351 108575 0676 (ACARS Reply)

Second message:

DDLXCXA CHIAK CHI68R

CHIAKUA 111351/ED

AGM

AN N591UA/GL FWA

UA93 EWRSFO

MESSAGE FROM CHIDD -

LAND ASP AT NEAREST -- NEAREST AIRPORT. ASP .ASP ON GROND. ANYWERE.

CHIDD ED BALLINGER

09111351 108575 0669 (ACARS Reply)

Third Message:

DDLXCXA CHIAK CHI68R

CHIAKUA 111410/ED

CMD

AN N591UA/GL CMI

QUCHIAKUA 1UA93 EWRSFO

MESSAGE FROM CHIDD -

DO NOT DIVERT TO DC AREA

CHIDD ED BALLINGER

<u>09111410 108575 0706</u> (ACARS Reply)


Fourth Message:

DDLXCXA CHIAK CHI68R

CHIAKUA 111410/ED

CMD

AN N591UA/GL CMI

QUCHIAKUA 1UA93 EWRSFO

MESSAGE FROM CHIDD -

DO NOT DIVERT TO DC AREA

CHIDD ED BALLINGER

<u>09111411 108575 0707</u> (ACARS Reply)


The first 8 digits in the ACARS reply are Date and Zulu time (GMT).These messages are based on Category A and B flight tracking. This aircraft would not have had messages routed through the above remote ground stations if it were en-route to crash in Shanksville, PA. Many other stations are much closer if in fact United 93 crashed in Shanksville. In order to follow the messages based on remote ground stations, the Pilots for Truth had included the Google Earth File used to construct the various stations and associated messages, with an overlay of the United 93 Flight path according to the National Transportation Safety Board.

There were many genuine witnesses to the crash of a plane at Indian Lake over a mile SE of the crash site. A lady described a small white plane and it coming over Shanksville near the crash site. She said the FBI asked her to describe it. It was a moulded craft and it banked and flew real low over trees towards the lake. She said it was about the size of a van, cylindrical in shape with lateral rear spoiler, smooth body and no rivets. The FBI said the plane was probably a Lear jet taking pictures. She replied, 'What, just before the crash?'

Another lady described it coming over her house near Indian Lake and then nipped the top of a tree. It had a 'terrible roaring noise'. The craft exploded over the lake according to several witnesses. The debris rained down over a considerable area. The witnesses at the sink hole, or mine shaft, told reporters there was no sign of the plane just a smoking hole and burnt trees with ATF agents walking about.

The crash damage was spread over several miles and when collected amounted to an insignificant amount of small debris. An engine was found a mile or so from the hole. Most of the debris found in the region of Indian Lake was no more than two or three miles from the sink-hole. The rough location of the exploded craft was in the area of Stonycreek near to Shanksville.

## Folk Lore

The legend of Flight 93 is now firmly established in folk lore. Lisa Beamer was present and honoured by President Bush in his speech to Congress shortly after 9/11. Tony Blair was also there and took credit from the President who thanked Britain for its support and reaffirmed the close friendship between the two countries. Mr. Bush also thanked many other countries including Pakistan for their condolences.

It is not for me as a loyal citizen to make a judgement if the facts be allowed to get in the way of an emotional appeal from my president to the world, for its support, against the intentions of some loose knit, wide ranging terrorist organisation with a central intelligence brain. However the beast is real and the devil is in the detail and the rest is politics which sweeps over us all like a catastrophic avalanche.

Ten cell phone calls of the fifteen calls were allegedly made from Fl 93 but the FBI later retracted this after the Zacarias Moussaoui trial. They decided that Tom Burnett did not call his wife Deena from his cell phone, he used a seat phone. But there were no seat phones on these aircraft according to the airlines. However she said his mobile number was recorded on her ID. They also said the terrorists had no gun but used a knife or box cutter(s), to help explain how the knife got past security no doubt. Deena was a flight attendant for Delta Airlines.

On Fl 77 the Ted Olsen's wife Barbara, a reporter on CNN, said his was only an attempted call that failed yet it was stated initially by the FBI that the call was made and the hijackers used box cutters. Ted Olsen-Solicitor General had influenced the Supreme Courts' decision against Al Gore in favour of Bush's election.

The FBI finally said only two calls in total were made when the planes descended, in all of the four events. Later it is generally admitted no calls at all were made from cell phones since it was technically impossible at high altitude. Also in all four flights no warning was given using the high jack code whereby any one pilot could simply hit the transponder button.

## Pristine Evidence

According to the 9/11 Commission, the passports of two of the hijackers of Flight 93 were found intact in the aircraft's debris field. The doctored passport of hijacker Abdul Aziz al Omari was found in Mohamed Atta's left-behind luggage. When examining this luggage, the FBI found important clues about the hijackers and their plans.

Atta's luggage contained papers that revealed the identity of all nineteen hijackers, and provided information about their plans, motives, and backgrounds. The FBI was able to determine details such as dates of birth, known and/or possible residences, visa status, and specific identity of the suspected pilots. None of these documents have been examined by independent legal experts.

The investigators soon linked the men to al Qaeda, from their agency files. The New York Times reported on September 12 that the authorities had identified accomplices in several cities who had helped plan the attacks. They prepared profiles of each and traced the recent movements of these men. FBI agents in Florida visited flight schools and places in pursuit of leads. At one flight school, students said investigators were there within hours of the attacks.

The Washington Post reported the FBI had combed their files on Satam al Suqami and Ahmed al Ghamdi. They noted the pair's ties to Nabil al Marabh and searched for him. On 9/11 they said bin Laden was responsible for the attacks. On September 27, 2001, they released photos of the suspects along with their details.

The abstract reveals how the FBI was able to prove the identity of the hijackers within a few days. However bizarre the evidence, it is taken as the unquestionable proof that Boeing aircrafts were piloted by amateurs to fly the planes and crash them, leaving evidence of intact passports yet not a scrap of evidence of the remains of dead people or titanium engines, because these masses had disintegrated.

This has to be the most blatant account of a zany plot in history especially in the extent and amount of resources used to convince the public of a diabolical plot by Islamic fundamentalists against the most defended nation on earth. Yet it still worked, because of our free international press.

# Chapter 14

## Oil, War and Regime Change

*We can't change the laws of Physics but we might be able to bend them a little to satiate our need for more energy.*

According to the Iraq Inquiry, MI6 foresaw the overthrow of Saddam over a year before the assault on Iraq in 2003, classified papers revealed. They offered a plan that was layered like an onion, with ministers backing regime change whilst secretly working with Sunni factions to affect a rebellion.

The spy service made it clear in newly released papers that the award for deposing the Iraqi dictator was security to oil supplies. The documents reveal this is the reason U.S. and Britain went to war, and not because they feared Saddam possessed weapons of mass destruction. The inquiry heard that Tony Blair was willing to back regime change when he met

George Bush in Texas in 2002. But the latest papers point out how the removal of Saddam had been debated by the inner cabinet months earlier.

The head of MI6 sent three documents to Mr Blair's top foreign policy adviser Sir David Manning in December 2001. Two discussed how Britain could try and prevent the U.S. from invading Iraq. But the other set out a route map for regime change very openly. An MI6 officer known only as SIS4 told Manning: 'At our meeting on 30 November we discussed how we could combine an objective of regime change in Baghdad with the need to protect important regional interests which would be at grave risk.'

He suggested a timetable for the plan to work to meet U.S. impatience for the removal of Saddam. But he warned them: 'Government law officers to provide assurances of legality; there has been a serious problem here.'

In the third document to Manning, the intelligence officer warned that an invasion of Iraq would not be as easy as the initial coalition thrust into Afghanistan. 'The defences of the Iraqi regime are formidable. The Tikritis are not a bunch of Taliban.' But he said an invasion could boost support for terrorism, increase distrust of the U.S. and its allies in the Islamic world and raise oil prices. Manning advised it was because the ties between Iraq and the terror atrocities were being discussed in the U.S.

## We're running out of Energy

In May of 2001, Bush said, after meeting with Secretary of Defence Wolfowitz & Secretary of Energy - Spencer Abraham: 'What people need to hear loud and clear, is that we're running out of energy in America.' It urged Bush to establish in January of 2001, the National Energy Policy Development Group. The task force was headed by Dick Cheney to develop a long range plan to meet US energy requirements.

It was Rense.com that revealed Enron's arrangement with Halliburton to build a multi-billion dollar oil pipeline through Afghanistan and the ensuing failed negotiations with the Taliban prior to 9/11. When in July of 2001, the negotiations between Enron, Halliburton, the US government and the Taliban failed due to the Taliban's rejection of terms, the US negotiators warned the Taliban, saying, 'either you accept our offer of a carpet of gold, or we bury you under a carpet of bombs'. ['Bin Laden, La Verite Interdite.' (Bin Laden, the Forbidden Truth) by Jean-Charles Brisard and Guillaume Dasquie-2001].

One of the signers of the NEPDG was Bush's Secretary of the Treasury, Paul O'Neill. He later revealed that due to its vast oil reserves, Iraq had become an objective to Cheney and Bush at the outset. O'Neill was outspoken, often against the administration's party line. He stated the United States faced a budget deficit of more than US $500 billion.

So as to outline his own legacy during his final days in office, Bush avowed that the US military is greater than what he had inherited. 'We must take the fight to our enemies across the world,' Bush told an audience of West Point cadets on December 9, 2008. 'We've laid a foundation, upon which future presidents and future military leaders can build.'

Patrick Buchanan takes Bush to task for getting the US bogged down in two costly wars:

'Two-thirds of Americans now believe that the Iraq war was a mistake. What turned Americans against the war was the long, costly, bloody slog, now in its fifth year, with nearly 5,000 of our soldiers dead. The war in Afghanistan too, after we failed to capture bin Laden or to create a democratic Afghanistan. We are entering the eighth year of the war yet the Taliban grows stronger and victory is further away than ever.'

## The Countdown to War

Bush said from the start that Saddam was a bad person and needed to be removed - go find me a way to do this. In April 2001 the CIA were trying to implicate Iraq by getting false evidence from the Iraqi Envoys in New York, by open threats, according to Susan Lindauer. Instead Iraq was offering massive trade options if the UN would lift the sanctions. Bin Laden was ill in Dubai and with his pro-Saudi connections would help to create the 9/11 deception and then blame this billionaire warlord.

This had been pre-planned already with the US and British already making troop movements six months ahead of 9/11. The following news briefs and intelligence gives the knowledge that both Afghanistan and Iraq were prime targets with Allied troop movements into Oman (200 miles from Afghanistan across the Arabian Sea via Pakistan) and satellite Eurasian countries well before 9/11. Then after 9/11 Rumsfeld stated both countries would be considered enemies of the US.

According to Paul Thompson the US was preparing for war well before 9/11, with increasing control of Asia before and since and suggestions of advanced knowledge that an attack would take place on or around 9/11. In 1996 the Institute for Advanced Strategic and Political Studies, a pro- Israeli think tank, publishes a paper entitled 'A Clean Break: A New Strategy for Securing the Realm.'

The paper is right-wing and pro-Zionist; the lead writer was Richard Perle chairman of the Defence Policy Board in the US, and very influential with Bush. The paper advises the new Israeli leader Binyamin Netanyahu to adopt a strategy that restores strategic initiative and vigour, through Zionism. The first stage would be the removal of Saddam Hussein. A war with Iraq would undermine the Middle East, allowing regimes in Syria, Iran and Lebanon to be replaced.

In 1997 the former National Security Advisor Zbigniew Brzezinski depicts Eurasia as strategic to world power and Central Asia with its vast oil reserves as the key to this strategy. He states that for the US to maintain its global power, it must control that area. In his book 'The Grand Chessboard: American Primacy and its Geostrategic Imperatives', Brzezinski reasons that the public will resist US military expansion and that his Central Asian strategy might not be realised except in the event of a perceived external threat. Brzezinski was a consultant backing Amoco in the partnership with Bridas that had the initial contracts with Turkmenistan for the oil pipe line.

It is claimed that CIA paramilitary teams start entering Afghanistan in Nov 2001. It is revealed in 1998 by Uzbekistan that they and the US have been conducting joint covert operations against Afghanistan's Taliban regime and bin Laden since before 1998. [Times of India, 10/14/01; Washington Post, 10/14/01].

In 1999 The CIA finds an abandoned airstrip in Afghanistan, and makes plans to use it to evacuate a captured bin Laden, take agents in and out, and similar purposes. It is a joint project run by the CIA and NSA. [Washington Post, 12/19/01].

CIA Director Tenet later claims that in 1999, the CIA established a network of agents throughout Afghanistan and other countries aimed at capturing bin Laden and his deputies. [UPI, 10/17/02].

Tenet states that by 9/11, 'a map would show that these human networks were in place in such numbers to nearly cover Afghanistan. This array meant that, when the military campaign to topple the Taliban and destroy al Qaeda began in October 2001, we were able to support it with an enormous body of information and a large stable of assets.' [Senate Intelligence Committee, 10/17/02].

On March 3, 1999. The Executive Director of the Centre for Strategy before the Senate Armed Services Subcommittee: 'There is a need to transform the US military into a different kind of force. Without a strong external shock to the United States - a latter-day Pearl Harbour of sorts - transformation will likely prove a long one.' [CSBA, 3/5/99].

Early 2000: The US has established significant military-to-military relationships with Kyrgyzstan, Uzbekistan and Kazakhstan. Their armies have an ongoing relationship with the National Guard of three US states - Kazakhstan with Arizona, Kyrgyzstan with Montana, and Uzbekistan with Louisiana. The countries also participate in NATO's Partnership for Peace program. [Washington Post, 8/27/02].

September 2000: The neo-conservative think tank Project for the New American Century writes a blueprint for the creation of a global Pax Americana. The document, entitled Rebuilding America's Defences: Strategies, Forces and Resources for a New Century, was written for the Bush team even before the 2000 Presidential election. It was commissioned by

Cheney, Rumsfeld, Wolfowitz, Jeb Bush and Cheney's future Chief of Staff Lewis Libby.

The report is a blueprint for global US pre-eminence, in line with American principles and interests. The Bush administration intended to take military control of the Persian Gulf oil despite Saddam Hussein and would retain control of the region. It also says: The United States has for decades sought to play a more permanent role in Gulf regional security. While the unresolved conflict with Iraq provides the immediate justification, the need for a substantial American force presence in the Gulf transcends the issue of the regime of Saddam Hussein. The report calls for the control of space through a new 'US Space Forces', the political control of the internet, the subversion of any growth in political power of even close allies, and advocates regime change in China, North Korea, Libya, Syria, Iraq and Iran.

It also says that biological warfare that can target specific genotypes may transform biological warfare from the realm of terror to a politically useful tool. However, the report complains that these changes are likely to take a long time, 'absent some catastrophic and catalysing event - like a new Pearl Harbour.' [PNAC Report, 8/00].

A British Member of Parliament says of the report: 'This is a blueprint for US world domination - a new world order of their making. These are the thought processes of fantasist Americans who want to control the world.' [Sunday Herald, 9/7/02].

December 19, 2000: The Washington Post reports that the United States has quietly begun to align itself with those in the Russian government calling for military action against Afghanistan and has toyed with the idea of a new raid to wipe out bin Laden. Russia and the US are debating what kind of government should replace the Taliban. The US was talking about the overthrow of a regime that controls most of the country, in the hope it can be replaced with a supposed government that does not exist even on paper. It appears that all pre-9/11 plans to invade Afghanistan involve attacking from the north with Russia, but 9/11 allows the US to do it without Russian help.

January 21, 2001: George Bush Jr. is inaugurated as the 43$^{rd}$ US President, replacing Clinton. The major figure to remain in office is CIA Director Tenet, appointed in 1997 and a long-time friend of Bush senior. FBI Director Louis Freeh stays on until June 2001. Numerous figures in Bush's administration are in the oil industry, including Bush, Vice President Cheney and National Security Advisor Rice. Enron's ties also reach deep into the administration.

March 15, 2001: The US is working with India, Iran, and Russia in a concerted front against Afghanistan's Taliban. India is supplying the Northern Alliance with military equipment, advisers and helicopter technicians and both India and Russia are using bases in Tajikistan and Uzbekistan for their operations. [Jane's Intelligence Review, 3/15/01].

Spring 2001: The Sydney Morning Herald later reports: The months preceding 9/11, sees a shifting of the US military's focus. Starting in April 2001 a series of military documents is released that seek to legitimize the use of US military force in the pursuit of oil and gas.

An article in the Army War College's journal by Jeffrey Record, a former staff member of the Senate armed services committee, argues for the legitimacy of shooting in the Persian Gulf on behalf of lower gas prices. He also advocates presidential subterfuge in the promotion of conflict and urges disguising the US's reasons for warfare with chivalry, to get public support for a war.

In April, Tommy Franks the commander of US forces in the Persian Gulf and South Asia area testifies to Congress in April that his command's key mission is access to the region's energy resources. The next month US Central Command begins planning for war with Afghanistan, plans that are later used in the real war. [Sydney Morning Herald, 12/26/02].

April 2001: A report commission by former US Secretary of State James Baker entitled 'Strategic Energy Policy Challenges for The 21$^{st}$ Century' is submitted to Vice President Cheney this month. The American people continue to demand cheap energy without sacrifice or inconvenience. The US remains a prisoner of its energy dilemma and needs to invade Iraq to secure its oil supply. [Sunday Herald, 10/5/02].

In Afghanistan, the report suggests the US should investigate changes to US policy to export more oil from the Caspian Basin region if an economical export route could be identified swiftly.

May 16, 2001: US General Tommy Franks, later to head the US occupation of Afghanistan, visits the capital of Tajikistan. He says the Bush administration considers Tajikistan a strategically significant country and offers military aid. The Guardian later asserts that by this time, US Rangers were also training special troops in Kyrgyzstan. There were unconfirmed reports that Tajik and Uzbek special troops were training in Alaska and Montana.

June 2001: China, Russia and four Central Asian countries create the Shanghai Cooperation Organization. Its explicit purpose is to oppose US dominance, especially in Central Asia. [Guardian, 10/23/01].

June 26, 2001: An Indian magazine reports more details of the cooperative efforts of the US, India, Russia, Tajikistan and Uzbekistan and Iran against the Taliban regime: 'India and Iran will facilitate US and Russian plans for military action against the Taliban. Earlier in the month, Russian President Putin told a meeting of the Confederation of Independent States that military action against the Taliban may happen, possibly with Russian involvement using bases and forces from Uzbekistan and Tajikistan as well. [India Reacts, 6/26/01].

July 15, 2001: Members of the G8 countries, in Genoa, Italy for an upcoming G8 summit discuss the Taliban, the Afghanistan pipeline, and the handing over of bin Laden. According to Pakistani representative Ambassador Niaz Naik, the US delegation, led by former Clinton Ambassador to

Pakistan, Tom Simmons warns of a military option if the Taliban doesn't change its attitude. [Bin Laden: The Forbidden Truth. Guillaume Dasquié and Jean-Charles Brisard].

July 21, 2001: Three American officials, Tom Simmons, Karl Inderfurth (former Assistant Secretary of State for South Asian Affairs) and Lee Coldren (former State Department expert on South Asia) meet with Pakistani and Russian intelligence officers in a Berlin hotel. It is the third back-channel conference called brainstorming on Afghanistan. The Taliban sat in on previous meetings, but rejected this one due to worsening tensions. The ISI relays information to the Taliban. [Guardian, 9/22/01].

At the meeting Coldren passes on a message from Bush officials as the US was considering military action. Niaz Naik is told by American officials that military action against the Taliban is planned before the snows started falling in Afghanistan, by the middle of October at the latest. The goal is to kill or capture bin Laden and Taliban leader Mullah Omar; topple the Taliban regime and install a transitional government of moderate Afghans in its place. Uzbekistan and Russia would also participate. Naik also says Washington would not drop its plan even if bin Laden were to be surrendered immediately by the Taliban. [Guardian, 9/26/01].

One specific threat made at this meeting is that the Taliban can choose between carpets of bombs - an invasion - or carpets of gold - the pipeline. [Bin Laden: The Forbidden Truth, Guillaume Dasquié and Jean-Charles Brisard].

Late summer 2001: The Guardian later reports: Reliable western military sources say a US contingency plan existed on paper by the end of the summer to attack Afghanistan from the north. [Guardian, 9/26/01].

August 6, 2001: Richard Perle, head of the Defence Policy Board and foreign policy advisor to Bush, is asked about new challenges now that the Cold War is over. He cites three: Iraq, North Korea and Iran. [Australian Broadcasting Corp., 8/6/01].

Note that these three nations are the same three named in Bush's famous January 2002 axis of evil speech. US officials talk about attacking all three but they have no links to al-Qaeda. [Newsweek, 8/11/02].

Mid-August 2001: Mujahidin leader Abdul Haq returns to Peshawar, Pakistan from the US. With support from the US, he launches subversive operations in Afghanistan. [Wall Street Journal, 11/2/01].

Abdul is later killed entering Afghanistan in October 2001, after his position is betrayed to the Taliban by the ISI. [Toronto Star, 11/5/01].

September 4, 2001: Bush's Cabinet-rank advisers have their second ever meeting on terrorism. Back in January, terrorism czar Richard Clarke had proposed an ambitious plan to roll back al-Qaeda's operations around the world. It was finally approved at this meeting. It now aims to eliminate it altogether. The plan calls for significant support to the Northern Alliance, the last remaining resistance to the Taliban in Afghanistan. At the same time, the US military would launch air strikes on training camps and special-operations missions in Afghanistan.

The plan was awaiting Bush's signature on 9/11. Clinton's limited missile attack in 1998 faced a lot of controversy - this new ambitious plan would have faced much more opposition had it not been for 9/11. A senior Bush administration official dismisses the allegations: This idea that there was somehow a kind of - some sort of full-blown plan for going after al-Qaeda is just incorrect. [CNN, 8/5/02].

September 9, 2001: A formal National Security Presidential Directive describing a 'game plan to remove al-Qaeda from the face of the Earth' is placed on Bush's desk for his signature. The plan deals with all aspects of a war against al-Qaeda, ranging from diplomatic initiatives to military operations in Afghanistan. According to NBC News reporter Jim Miklaszewski, the directive outlines essentially the same war plan to be put into action after the 9/11 attacks. The administration was able to respond quickly to the attacks because 9/11 was pre-planned. It included persuading the Taliban to turn over bin Laden and military invasion.

It was prepared through a process of consultation over many months, involving the Pentagon, CIA, State Department and other security and intelligence agencies. Bush was expected to sign the directive, but hadn't finished reviewing it by 9/11. [NBC News, 5/16/02, Los Angeles Times, 5/18/02].

September 11, 2001. The 9/11 attack: four planes are allegedly hijacked, two crash into the WTC, one into the Pentagon, and one crashes into the Pennsylvania countryside.

September 11, 2001: Hours after the 9/11 attacks, Defence Secretary Rumsfeld is given information that three of the names on the airplane passenger manifests are suspected al Qaeda operatives. The notes he composes at the time are leaked nearly a year later. Rumsfeld writes he wants the 'best info [sic] fast. Judge whether good enough and hit Saddam Hussein at same time. Not only bin Laden. Go massive. Sweep it all up. Things related and not.' [CBS, 9/4/02].

He presents the idea to Bush the next day. It is later revealed that shortly after 9/11, Rumsfeld sets up a small team of defence officials outside regular intelligence channels to focus on unearthing details about Iraqi ties with al Qaeda and other terrorist networks. And they continued to sift through much of the same databases available to government intelligence analysts with the aim of spotlighting information the spy agencies have either overlooked or played down. [Washington Post, 10/25/02].

September 12, 2001: 9/11 should be blamed on Iraq and not just al Qaeda. Rumsfeld proposes to Bush that Iraq should be a main target in the war against terrorism. Wolfowitz and others support the idea. Bush and his advisors agree that Iraq should be attacked, but they decide to wait. Secretary of State Powell says, 'Public opinion has to be prepared before a move against Iraq.' [Washington Post, 1/28/02, Los Angeles Times, 1/12/03].

September 15, 2001: CIA Director Tenet briefs Bush with top-secret plans, the culmination of four years of work on bin Laden, the al-Qaeda network and worldwide terrorism. Tenet advocates a strategy to create a northern front, closing the safe haven of Afghanistan. His idea is that Afghan opposition forces, aided by the US, would move first against the northern city of Mazar-i-Sharif, try to break the Taliban's grip on that city and free the border with Uzbekistan. From there the campaign could move to other cities in the north.

Tenet also explains that CIA had begun working with a number of tribal leaders to stir up resistance in the south the previous year. The military strategy that transpired had been prepared by the CIA over the past four years. Tenet used a top secret document called the Worldwide Attack Matrix, which described covert operations in eighty countries. The actions ranged from propaganda to lethal covert action in preparation for military attacks. The military, the usual planner of military campaigns, was relatively unready and deferred to the CIA plans. [Washington Post, 1/31/02].

September 15 - November 1, 2001: Two of the largest war games in history take place during the build-up for war in Afghanistan. Both have been planned several years in advance. Operation Swift Sword 2, the biggest deployment of British troops since the

Falklands War, sends 22,000 British troops to Oman, a country 200 miles from Pakistan. It ran from September 15 to October 26. [News Ahead, 9/1/01].

Meanwhile, 23,000 US troops take part in Operation Bright Star, from October 8 to November 1. In Egypt, they join 50,000 soldiers from Egypt, Britain, France, Germany, Greece, Italy, Spain, Jordan and Kuwait for what is possibly the largest war game of all time. At the same time two US carrier battle groups arrive on station in the Gulf of Arabia just off the Pakistani coast. Other reports suggest the US was planning a war in Afghanistan for mid-October.

September 17, 2001: President Bush signs a document marked 'Top Secret' that outlines a plan for going to war in Afghanistan. The document also directs the Pentagon to begin planning military options for an invasion of Iraq. Two days after Bush signs the document, the Defence Policy Board - with Rumsfeld in attendance - meets at the Pentagon and discusses the ousting of Saddam Hussein (a policy Perle had advocated in 1996 for rebuilding Zionism). Iraq secretly becomes a central focus of the US's counter-terrorism efforts over the next nine months, without much internal debate, public pronouncements or paper trail. [Washington Post, 1/12/02].

September 21, 2001: A secret report to NATO allies says the US wants to hear allied views on post-Taliban Afghanistan after the liberation of the country. However, the US is publicly claiming it will not overthrow the Taliban. [Guardian, 9/21/01].

Late September-Early October 2001: The leaders of Pakistan's two Islamic parties negotiate bin Laden's extradition to Pakistan to stand trial for 9/11. Bin Laden would be held under house arrest in Peshawar and would face an international tribunal, to decide whether to try him or hand him over to the US. According to reports in Pakistan, this plan has the approval of Taliban leader Mullah Omar. The plan is vetoed by Pakistan's president Musharraf who says he could not guarantee bin Laden's safety. It appears the US did not want the deal: a US official later says that casting our objectives too narrowly risked a premature collapse of the international effort to overthrow the Taliban if by some lucky chance bin Laden was captured. [Mirror, 7/8/02].

October 5, 2001: 1,000 US soldiers are sent to the Central Asian nation of Uzbekistan, which borders Afghanistan. [AP, 8/19/02].

October 15, 2001: According to the Moscow Times, Russia sees the possible US conquest of Afghanistan as an attempt by the US to replace Russia as the dominant political force in Central Asia, with the control of oil as a prominent motive. They say the bombardment of Afghanistan outwardly appears to hinge on issues of fundamentalism and American retribution. Underneath lurks the prize of the energy-rich Caspian basin into which oil majors have invested billions of dollars. Ultimately, this war will set the boundaries of US and Russian influence in Central Asia and determine the future of oil and gas resources of the Caspian Sea. [Moscow Times, 10/15/01].

December 19, 2001: Speaking in Kazakhstan, US Assistant Secretary of State Elizabeth Jones states: We will not leave Central Asia after resolving the conflict in Afghanistan. We want to support the Central Asian countries in their desire to reform their societies as they supported us in the war against terrorism. These are not only new but long-term relations. [BBC, 12/19/01]. This important change in official US policy is not reported in the US.

January 16, 2002: It is reported that US bases in the Central Asian nations of Kyrgystan and Uzbekistan, originally agreed as temporary and emergency expedients, are now permanent. More airfields are under US control in Tajikistan and Pakistan. [Guardian, 1/16/02].

March 30, 2002: With US troops already in many Central Asian countries, it is now reported that US Special Forces soldiers are training Kazakhstan troops in a secret location. [London Times, 3/30/02].

April 11, 2002: In a speech, Jim Pavitt, the CIA Deputy Director of Operations says the CIA intends to launch subversive actions in Afghanistan immediately after 9/11: 'With a small logistical footprint they came with lightning speed. They came with knowledge of local languages, whatever you heard to the contrary notwithstanding, terrain, and politics. In those few days my officers stood on Afghan soil, side by side with Afghan friends that we had developed over a long period of time, and we launched America's war against al-Qaeda. Quite simply, we were there well before the 9/11.' [CIA, 4/11/02].

This contrasts with the usual story in the media that the US overly relied on satellites and other communications, and had no agents on the ground. Yet again in May 2002 Rumsfeld was so determined to find reason for an attack that, on ten separate occasions, he asked the CIA to find evidence linking Iraq to the terror attacks of 9/11. They failed to do so. [Time, 5/6/02].

July 10, 2002: A briefing given to a top Pentagon advisory group states: The Saudis are active at every level of the terror chain, from planners to financiers, from cadre to foot-soldier, from ideologist to cheerleader. Saudi Arabia supports our enemies and attacks our allies. They are called the kernel of evil, the prime mover, and the most dangerous opponent.

This position still runs counter to official US policy, but the Washington Post says it represents a point of view that has growing currency within the Bush administration. The briefing suggests that the Saudis be given an ultimatum to stop backing terrorism or face seizure of its oil fields and its financial assets invested in the United States. The group, the Defence Policy Board, is headed by Richard Perle. [Washington Post, 8/6/02].

An international controversy follows the public reports of the briefing in August. In an abrupt change, the media starts calling the Saudis enemies, not allies of the US. Slate reports details of the briefing the Post failed to mention. The briefing states, there is an Arabia, but it needs not be Saudi. The Grand strategy for the Middle East is: Iraq is the tactical pivot. Saudi Arabia is the strategic pivot. Egypt is the prize. [Slate, 8/7/02]. Note that a similar meeting of the Defence Policy Board appears to have preceded and affected the US decision to take a warlike stance against Iraq.

July 16, 2002: British Prime Minister Tony Blair said: 'We knew about al Qaeda for a long time. They were committing terrorist acts, they were planning, and they were organizing. Everybody knew, we all knew, that Afghanistan was a failed state living on drugs and terror. We did not act. To be truthful about it, there was no way we could have got the public consent to have suddenly launched a campaign on Afghanistan but for what happened on 9/11.' [London Times, 7/17/02].

It was brilliant intelligence for Mr. Blair. Afghanistan was living on drugs and terror. Afghan farmers were processing poppies from their necessary to survive crops, just like tobacco. The Taliban were in league with al Qaeda and bin Laden who were planning and organising the downfall of the US by attacking New York and Washington. So the US then staged a never ending war on terror. Unfortunately the British government was by then already programmed to go to war alongside its young partner and super power.

August 16, 2002: The commander of US forces in Afghanistan says US troops will remain there for a long, long time. He likens the situation to South Korea, where US soldiers have been for over 50 years. [AP, 8/16/02].

August 25, 2002: General Tommy Franks, head of the US Central Command, suggests that the war on terror should not be limited to Afghanistan, but expand into neighbouring countries as well. [Reuters, 8/25/02].

August 27, 2002: The Central Asian nation of Uzbekistan has recently signed a treaty committing the US to respond to any external threat to the country. Uzbekistan's foreign minister: The logic of it all suggests that the United States has come here with a serious purpose, and for a long time. The other Central Asian nations - Kazakhstan, Kyrgyzstan, Tajikistan, and Turkmenistan - have similar agreements with the US. The US claims it is supporting democracy in these nations, but experts say authoritarianism has been on the rise since 9/11. A new US military base in Uzbekistan currently holds about 1,000 US soldiers, but is being greatly enlarged. The article makes out the US is replacing Russia as the dominant power in Central Asia. [Washington Post, 8/27/02].

The foregoing reports across the spectrum show how the US was preparing the ground work to invade not just Afghanistan and Iraq but a number of Middle East countries. And in parallel Saudi Arabia had been their stalwart supporter in the Gulf war. See the book 'Desert Warrior' by HRH General Khaled Bin Sultan. House of Saud, Co-Commander of Joint Forces in Gulf War 1991. Indeed the biggest reason for US militarism stems from the stated Bush Energy Policy - that America needs much of the world's oil resources to sustain its own insatiable demands. The serpent will eat its tail.

That Russia might appear to support its old enemy could be for them to ostensibly work together in controlling the vacuum created by the break-up of the Soviet Union; but these regimes are becoming more authoritarian, in hoc to the US and trading their resources, just like the CIA infiltration and set up of old puppet military regimes in South America to replace more liberal socialist leaders like Allende with ruthless tyrants like Pinochet in Chile.

# CHAPTER 15

## Raison D'etre

### All good things come to an End, including life.

We cannot be exactly certain about the list of casualties in the events on 9/11 in NY, if many or hopefully very few. The Social Security Administration records show no change in the average numbers of State deaths in New York State and New Jersey for September 11th 2001. This in itself indicates that the media quoted death count is totally wrong whatever their source and there was a total lack on film, of dead body close ups. The videos and stills for the North Tower jumpers exhibited heavy pixilation and the videos images of moving arms were distortions. Also the videos of the planes showed how they entered the buildings without deformation.

The plane shots showed faded blue/grey backgrounds when compared with the real background shots that had no images of the planes. The videos showed the plane disappearing behind the South Tower before the separate explosion in the front view. The fake videos were composites that show the image of a plane going through the tower intact, with no crash debris or deformation on entering the towers. The Fox News-Chopper 5 live video showed the nose cone emerging intact from the South Tower. It was then doctored into flames, for the evening news.

Of the 19 hijackers many were proven to be still alive. The FBI has admitted the cell phone calls from the aircraft were not possible. There is no satisfactory explanation for the mysterious destruction of WTC 7 as the 9/11 Commission failed to mention it in their final report. The general view is that it was caused by fire but how could a fire bring a 47 storey building down in six seconds. It was reported as having fallen by Reuters to the BBC, 20 minutes before it did fall. And most people have never even heard of the fate of Building 6 - the Custom's House destruction - its core disappeared leaving a shell, along with the near total destruction of buildings 3, 4 and 5.

There was no evidence of phones, desks, filing cabinets, computers, carpets or bodies from the towers and no massive titanium engines or passenger seats.

There were no bodies found by the coroner at Shanksville because the white jet exploded over Indian Lake about a mile or two from the smoking hole in the ground. The transponder signals confirmed the real locations of UA175 and UA93 as being over Pennsylvania and then finally landing at John Hopkins Airport in Cleveland as confirmed by a spokesman for United Airlines at the time.

At the Pentagon a white jet crashed near the west wall at 9.32 before the two massive explosions, between 9.37 and 10.10 am. The Transport Secretary Norman Mineta stated that Cheney, in the underground bunker of the White House, allowed the military jet to keep on heading for the Pentagon at ten miles and closing fast before it crashed into hundreds of small pieces near the helipad.

There were thousands of Put options on Wall St on United and American Airlines exposed by Stock Exchange experts. The reason given - it must have been bin Laden's insider traders. Also there were stock falls on Lehman Brothers, Morgan Stanley, Cantor Fitzgerald, Merrill Lynch, American Express and others with empty offices in the Twin Towers.

The later videos of bin Laden on inspection appeared to be faked. Le Figaro reported he was in hospital in

Dubai suffering from kidney disease in July 2001. He was allegedly buried at sea in May 2011 yet no real evidence was produced and no sailors witnessed it on the Carl Vincent, except for senior officers. On 9/11 he was in hospital in Rawalpindi, Pakistan protected by the military. Fox News had reported his death in December 2001 from a kidney related or lung disease. They got this news from the Pakistan Observer.

FEMA's Search and Rescue Teams were already there on 9/11 with a massive dumper truck convoy before the towers fell. The gold bullion millions were removed before the towers fell. Seven hundred tiny bone splinters were 'found' on the roof of the Deutsche building five years later suggesting the total disintegration of hundreds of people, yet no other body parts were ever found.

Finally no one was sacked; indeed they were promoted. The media anchor men immediately implanted the idea the towers were brought down 'on purpose' because the buildings 'had collapsed' as a result of a 'suicidal terrorist attack' and that planes had 'smashed into the towers' and it was 'obviously a suicidal terrorist attack' and then citing 'terrorism' and 'Osama bin Laden' as the possible cause of attack.

## The Unthinkable

The buildings WTC 1, 2 and 7, to be rigged, needed to be emptied of fabrics and evacuated beforehand to ensure safety and for a symmetrical collapse. Also WTC 3, 4, 5, 6 and 7 plus the Deutsche Bank were all evacuated according to the press. WTC 7 was brought down in a controlled fashion as stated by Senator John Kerry, so by definition all personnel would have to be evacuated and this was officially confirmed.

It is unthinkable that any rational Government would allow demolition of buildings without the normal safety checks to prevent any real loss of life, be it VIP directors or even ordinary managers and staff. This must have been the case, from the lack of real visual evidence of any dead people.

At the Pentagon there were no bodies, because of the statement 'no bodies were found from the Boeing crash because they were totally disintegrated'. The photographic evidence alone shows the plane crash was a military jet or UAV that crashed near Wedge 2 of the West wall and no dead pilot was found here (29).

Inside the Pentagon there were dead bodies recorded officially in the Pentagon Report but the Pentagon

Autopsy (AFIP) report did not confirm any independent evidence of DNA results. The remains were said to be incinerated and the ashes were said to have been transported to the Dover landfill in Delaware. And the public did not see any evidence nor did they see any body bags (33). Any real material evidence was impounded by the FBI and people were silenced from speaking out. All we see on photographs is several people alive on stretchers.

Two firemen outside the Pentagon were nearly injured when the plane crashed, since the jet crashed 150 feet north of the intended strike point. Also April Gallop and her colleagues inside the building on the ground floor were not injured.

There were quite a number of reported deaths of leading service personnel including John Patrick O'Neill - head of WTC Security, site manager Frank De Martini, Fire Chief Peter Ganci, Rev. Mychal Judge, Betty Ong, Barbara Olsen, David Angell and his wife and five Raytheon staff and many firemen, police, rescuers and of course the passengers, pilots and crew of the Boeings. These included Captain Charles Burlingame of Flight 77; Captain John Ogonowski the pilot and Thomas McGuinness the co-pilot of Flight 11; Captain Victor Saracini and

First Officer Michael Horrocks of Flight 175; Captain Jason Dahl of Flight 93. And finally amongst many others - Edna Cintron - the lady in the Tower, but her tribute was prepared on 9th March 2001.

## A Kind of Summary

The following summary briefly outlines the overall decision making process and actions of the White House Administration in the leading up to the Invasion of Iraq in response to 9/11.

The plan to re-invade Iraq began in 1992 from Wolfowitz and then accepted by Bush junior in 2003. Wolfowitz by then was undersecretary of defence for policy, took the lead in drafting an internal set of military guidelines called Defence Planning Guidance. The draft reasoned for a new military and political strategy in a post-Cold War world. If America has to act alone, so be it. The White House ordered Defence Secretary Cheney to revise it. In the new draft, pre-emption and U.S. willingness to act alone was removed.

On Jan. 20, 1993 Bill Clinton became President and the Iraq Containment Policy continued. During the Clinton administration, Saddam repeatedly tested U.N. inspections and sanctions. In 1995, Saddam's alleged son-in-law, who was head of Iraq's WMD program, defected and told inspectors about Iraq's arsenal. The U.N. inspectors searched Iraq's main biological weapons plant and demolished the equipment and growth medium.

On Jan. 26, 1998 a group of neoconservatives, who had formed the Project for a New American Century, argue for a much stronger U.S. global leadership exercised through 'military strength and moral clarity.' In a letter to Clinton, the group warns that the policy of containing Iraq is insufficient. They wanted to start military action and remove Saddam Hussein from power. This had to be the aim of American foreign policy.

Earlier Wolfowitz had veered from the official line of the Clinton administration by denouncing Saddam Hussein at a period when Rumsfeld was offering the dictator help in his conflict with Iran. James Mann points out that quite a few neo-conservatives, like Wolfowitz, believed in democratic ideals from the philosopher Leo Strauss, that there is a moral duty to oppose tyrants. Rumsfeld and his deputy Wolfowitz had written to Bill Clinton in 1998 urging war against Iraq and the removal of Saddam Hussein because he is a hazard to the world's oil supply.

The letter's signatories include Don Rumsfeld, Paul Wolfowitz, Richard Perle, William Kristol, and other future members of George W. Bush's administration, including Deputy Secretary of State, Richard Armitage and Under Secretary of State for Arms Control, John Bolton. These were known collectively as the Vulcans.

In Oct. 1998 Saddam stopped the weapons inspections. Then in November, Clinton during the Monica Lewinsky scandal ordered a bombing campaign against Iraq, but called it off when U.N. Secretary-General Kofi Annan got a deal in which Iraq promised to unconditionally cooperate with U.N. inspectors.

On Dec. 16-19, 1998 Operation Desert Fox began with U.S. and British military forces launching a four-day air and cruise missile campaign against approximately one hundred key Iraqi military targets to punish Saddam for defying U.N. weapons inspections. On Dec. 16, the day the bombing began, the U.N. withdrew all weapons inspectors. Inspections did not resume in Iraq until November 2002, following passage of U.N. Security Council Resolution 1441.

On Jan. 20, 2001 the second Bush Presidency began. Both hawks and realists present Bush with candidates for foreign policy posts in the new administration. The hawks end up with three important jobs: Lewis

Libby became Cheney's chief of staff, Don Rumsfeld became secretary of defence and Wolfowitz became his deputy. Colin Powell's nomination as secretary of state is viewed as a tough equalizer to the Pentagon hawks.

The two groups express varying views on how to deal with Saddam Hussein. The hawks develop a military option and push for increased aid to Iraqi opposition. Powell advocates 'smart sanctions' that would allow more humanitarian goods into Iraq, while tightening controls on items that could have military applications.

On the evening of 9/11, Mr. Bush threatens to punish those who harbour terrorists. Two days later, Wolfowitz builds on the president's maxim. He hints that the U.S. will expand its drive on terror to include Iraq. 'I think one has to say it's not just simply a matter of capturing people and holding them accountable, but removing the sanctuaries, removing the support systems and ending states who sponsor terrorism. And that's why it has to be a broad and sustained campaign.'

Colin Powell and others are stunned at Wolfowitz's rash views about ending states. Powell later responds during a press briefing. 'We're after ending terrorism.

And if there are states and regimes, nations that support terrorism, we hope to persuade them that it is in their interest to stop doing that. But I think ending terrorism is where I would like to leave it and let Mr. Wolfowitz speak for himself.'

Four days after the 9/11 attacks, Mr. Bush meets his national security team at Camp David for a council of war. Wolfowitz said now is the best time to act against state backers of terrorism, including Iraq. But Powell tells Bush that a UN coalition would unite for an attack on al Qaeda and the Taliban but not for an invasion of Iraq. The war council votes with Powell. Rumsfeld abstains. Mr. Bush eventually decides that the war's first phase will be Afghanistan. The question of Iraq will be reviewed later.

## Never Again

On Sept. 20, 2001 Mr. Bush addresses a Joint Session of Congress, building on his speech of 9/11. 'We will pursue nations that provide aid or safe haven to terrorism. Every nation, in every region, now has a decision to make. Either you are with us, or you are with the terrorists. From this day forward, any nation that continues to harbour or support terrorism will be regarded by the United States as a hostile regime.'

Mr. Bush's speech also sketches a picture for strong American leadership in the world, a leadership that would expand America's power and influence: 'Freedom and fear are at war. The advance of human freedom the great achievement of our time, and the great hope of every time now depends on us. Our nation, this generation, will lift a dark threat of violence from our people and our future. We will rally the world to this cause by our efforts, by our courage. We will not tire, we will not falter, and we will not fail.'

In Jan. 2002 the President's State of the Union address introduces the idea of an axis of evil that includes Iraq, Iran, and North Korea, and signals the U.S. will act pre-emptively to deal with such nations. 'North Korea is a regime arming with missiles and weapons of mass destruction, while starving its citizens. Iran aggressively pursues these weapons and exports terror. Iraq continues to flaunt its hostility toward America and to support terror. States like these, and their terrorist allies, constitute an axis of evil, arming to threaten the peace of the world. We'll be deliberate, yet time is not on our side. I will not wait on events, while dangers gather. I will not stand by, as peril draws closer and closer. The United States of America will not permit the world's most dangerous regimes to threaten us with the world's most destructive weapons.'

In June 2002 Mr. Bush outlines a Policy of Pre-emption. In a graduation speech at West Point, he cites the realities of a new post-Cold War era and outlines a major shift in national security strategy, from containment to pre-emption. 'Our security will require all Americans to be forward-looking and resolute, to be ready for pre-emptive action when necessary to defend our liberty and to defend our lives.' The president also calls for an American hegemony: 'America has, and intends to keep, military strengths beyond challenge.' Strategic aims, pre-emption and hegemony, echo the recommendations Wolfowitz made back in 1992 in his controversial Defence Planning Guidance draft.

In August 2002 at an Open Debate on Iraq in the chambers of the U.N. Security Council, Powell reports trouble getting U.S. allies on board for a war with Iraq and wants to consult the U.N. At a private dinner with Bush on Aug. 5, Powell warns the president that the U.S. should not act unilaterally and must fully consider the economic and political consequences of war, particularly in the Middle East. The Wall Street Journal argues that Bush junior is moving too quickly on Iraq and advocates pressing for the return of U.N. inspectors.

Vice President Cheney emerges as the Government voice backing action against Iraq. In Nashville speech to the Veterans of Foreign Wars, Cheney warns that 'a return of inspectors would provide no assurance whatsoever of Saddam's obedience with U.N. resolutions.' Cheney wants a longer term strategy whereby regime change in Iraq could transform the Middle East. 'Regime change in Iraq would bring about a number of benefits to the region. When the gravest of threats are eliminated, the freedom-loving peoples of the region will have a chance to promote the values that can bring lasting peace.'

On Sept. 12, 2002 in a United Nations speech, Bush seems to be with Powell in calling for a new U.N. resolution on Iraq. Bush also advised that 'The purposes of the United States should not be doubted. The Security Council resolutions will be enforced, the just demands of peace and security will be met or action will be unavoidable. And a regime that has lost its legitimacy will also lose its power.'

On Sept. 17, 2002 the U.S. National Security Strategy is delivered. The fundamentals of the Bush Doctrine are articulated in this paper. It presents a forward and comprehensive revision of U.S. overseas policy. It sketches a new and imperialistic American stance that will use pre-emption to deal with rogue states and terrorists holding weapons of mass destruction. It states that America will use its military and economic power to support free and open societies.

It will never again allow its military supremacy to be challenged as it was during the Cold War. The NSS paper asserts that when America's vital interests are at stake, it will act alone, if necessary.

Forget the Cost the Enemy are at the Gates

During his election campaign President Bush was against this kind of strategy but after 9/11 he listened to his pro-active hawk advisers led by Wolfowitz, Cheney, Kristol and Perle, the principle architects, to invade Iraq. Paul O'Neill the treasury secretary said Mr. Bush had become increasingly detached from economic reality and would not take advice that countered military invasions and should instead redress the looming US 500 billion dollar budget deficit.

On the early morning of 9/11, the Secretary of Defence spoke at a Pentagon breakfast meeting with members of Congress. According to his later story to

Larry King, he stated at the meeting that 'sometime in the next two months or so there would be an event that would occur in the world that would be sufficiently shocking that it would remind people again how important it is to have a strong healthy defence department that contributes to and underpins peace and stability in our world.'

Mr. Rumsfeld was never abashed at predicting shocking events within hours of their eventuality, nor in stating 2.3 trillion had gone missing the day before 9/11. Or better, in boasting of his predictions in the aftermath. This might help us understand how this particular event got its incredible source of squandered tax money - over four times the actual deficit that O'Neill said was essential to recover for America's future wellbeing. It would be enough to launch many more events in an 'endless' and insane war on terror paid for in reality by human blood and the death of innocents.

On the 30 Sept 2001 Attorney General John Ashcroft gave an outlandish warning that the United States faced another threat of more terrorism, and the risk will increase when the government launches avenger strikes. 'There is a clear and present danger to America. We believe there are others who would have plans and are pre-positioned to do things. I don't have any reason to believe that all those involved perished in the suicide attacks; and an unspecified number of other hijackings might have been planned,' Ashcroft said on CBS Face the Nation. He added: 'Federal agencies are gaining a better understanding of a vast global conspiracy rooted in Afghanistan, the base for the main suspect bin Laden. The deputy director of the CIA claimed that 'Many of the al Qaeda seniors still maintain that another crippling blow to New York City will cripple the United States.'

Using financial records, intercepted electronic communications and interviews with potential associates of the hijackers, the FBI had gathered evidence linking the suspects to a criminal web with outposts in Britain, Germany, Spain and the United Arab Emirates. Indeed, at the heart of some of our strongest allies.

In summary reflecting on the main reasons for the 9/11 event, apart from the re-generation of New York real estate was to justify pre-emptive wars in the interest of American geopolitical strategy in the Middle East and Central Asia and to secure vital oil supplies there. It had been conceived by the neo-cons even before the Clinton administration. But

Clinton may not have had any direct knowledge of it or possibly rejected it. The stage show required massive planning to include hundreds of participants and millions in pay offs. The decision to go ahead was made as soon as President Bush was advised and then convinced of the need to invade Iraq and Afghanistan in the interest of oil and resources under the guise of removing tyrants and terrorists.

Experts say it took around $500,000 to finance the attacks on 9/11. The money paid for the hijackers' extensive travel in the United States, training and living expenses during months of planning. They believe the money was moved from bases overseas to Florida, where many of the hijackers received pilot training, courtesy of the CIA. This is an insignificant cover amount to the true cost to the tax payers - estimated to be over four trillion dollars and rising and nothing compared to the death of innocents in the war on terror. The destruction of Iraq gave rise to Isis and its vengeful brigades, killing even more innocents. Iraq was destroyed just as the CIA predicted. And the cost to humanity and civilisation is beyond measure, East or West.

## The Good Die Young or True

Robin Cook resigned as Leader of the House in Blair's Government over Iraq. The gist of his speech was that Britain is being asked to embark on a war without the agreement of NATO, the European Union or the Security Council. The US can afford to go it alone, but Britain's interests are best protected not by unilateral action but by multilateral agreement and a world order governed by rules. France has been heavily criticised but Germany and Russia also want more time for inspections.

It is important to use the Security Council as the last hope of demonstrating international agreement. Neither the international community nor the British public think there is a compelling reason for invading Iraq. We cannot predict the death toll of civilians from the forthcoming bombardment of Iraq, but the US warning of a bombing campaign that will 'shock and awe' makes it likely that casualties will be very high. Iraq's military strength is far less than at the time of the last Gulf war. It is because Iraq is so weak that we can even contemplate its invasion. Britain's role in the Middle East is at odds with the Muslim world. Our credibility is damaged by our partners in Washington who are set on regime change in

Iraq. Any evidence that inspections may be showing headway is greeted in Washington with dismay. On Iraq, the British people want the inspections to continue and not to be pushed into a conflict by a US Administration with an agenda of its own. He voted against military action and resigned from the government in protest. Later this man of conscience was to die walking in the Scottish mountains. A UK veto would have left the US isolated from the UK, France, Germany, Russia, China, Canada, Australia and most of Europe. That Bush stated he would go it alone was another neo-con bluff. He really needed the political backing of the UK.

However plausible events like this appear to the public the creators meant to deceive us. In relating this story I have become an adversary of the neo-cons within my party believing them to be a prime cause of this plight by deception and the misery it has unleashed on the world well into the new millennium. The media and historians will continue to reinforce the grand deception as they did with President Lincoln and President Kennedy. The forces of good or evil are not relevant at the highest level of Government and its Intelligence services. Intelligence gets ever more funding under the guise of protecting the public and by playing the patriotism card. In effect this could lead to serious limitations on our civil rights and freedom of speech. This contradicts with the notion of a truly democratic nation. If most people are happy with this then so be it.

Socrates taught his students something whereby the balance of power is between good and evil in man and in his nature, yet to never lose sight of the essential reality of man in relation to morality, or of the human conscience in seeking justice and countering falsehoods and corruption. He was sentenced to death and chose to take hemlock poison.

The Hon. Abraham Lincoln stood for human rights and not deceit, in giving freedom. He wrote: 'As a result of the war, corporations have been enthroned, and an era of corruption in high places will follow, and the money power of the country will endeavour to prolong its reign by working on the prejudices of the people until all wealth is aggregated in a few hands, and the republic is destroyed. God grant that my suspicions may prove groundless.' He was martyred but the struggle to hang on to reality with a higher sense of moral purpose, over the 'vital interests' of the state, may yet prevail so that the Bill of Rights was not all for nothing. To end this story I will stay here living in the Polynesian Islands, sailing and fishing and learning of their customs. I try to paint like Paul Gaugin by copying his style. I am living in a thatched hut by a blue lagoon with beautiful native girls to paint but if Gauguin ever did forget Paris I will not forget New York. *The End*

# APPENDIX:
# REFERENCES FOR IMAGE SOURCES:
# GOOGLE IMAGES

Chapter 1. Sub-title: Al Qaeda: Page 9.

( 1 ) Intelligence file showing bin Laden's code name
http://www.alatoerka.nl/wpcontent/uploads/2010/11/
TimOsmanObl.gif

Subtitle: Quest for Oil: Page 12.

( 2 ) Bin Laden with Zbigniew Brezinski in 1986.
http://www.whale.to/b/alqaeda.html

Chapter 3. Subtitle: Black Ops: Page 77

( 3 ) The Craft did not detect the Barbed wire
http://www.alarabiya.net/articles/2011/06/15/153328.html

Chapter 6. Subtitle: Liquid Steel: Page 111

(4) Seismic Recordings at the Columbia Earth Institute
http://911research.wtc7.net/essays/gopm/indexg.html

Chapter 8. Subtitle: Cloak and Dagger: Page 123

(5) Mug Shots released by the FBI
http://911research.wtc7.net/cache/planes/evidence/
welfarestate_hijackers.html

Chapter 9: The Towers: Page 138

(6) The Confusion of Tongues: Engraving by
Gustave Dore 1865
http://www.artbible.info/images/
dore_toren_babel_grt.jpg

Subtitle: Structure: Page 145

(7) Dimensions of Core Columns and Spandrel plates
http://www.waarheid911.nl/twintowers.html

(8) Core structure of 47 columns. Outer shell of
240 columns

http://www.boweryboyshistory.com/2008/09/
minoru-yamasaki-man-who-made-twin.html

Subtitle: Preparations: Page 172

(9) Circa: 1973. In the sun's direct light the perimeter columns disappear. Without the sun the columns block out the day light.
http://architizer.com/blog/
new-york-citys-icons-under-construction/

Subtitle: Creative Artists: Page 174

(10) Exposed central core columns and elevator shafts plus details on 91$^{st}$ Floor of North Tower
http://www.markdotzler.com/Mark_Dotzler/
WTC_Artists.html

(11) Balcony Scene
http://www.conspiracy-cafe.com/apps/blog/
show/8636674-preparing-the-wtc-for-destruction

(12) The Trojan Contraption
http://www.markdotzler.com/Mark_Dotzler/
WTC_Artists.html

Chapter 10. Subtitle: Observations: Page 176

(13) Exploding debris from the south face of the South Tower
davidhandschuh.com/portfolio.php?c=sept11&i=1

(14) Edna Cintron Archive
http://m.actualno.com/curious/-471598.html

(15) Image of Lady
http://de.paperblog.com/die-3wahrheit-uber-911-145090/

(16) Image of a person falling from the North Tower
http://www.dailymail.co.uk/news/article-2035720/9-11-jumpers-America-wants-forget-victims-fell-Twin-Towers.html

(17) Some lower columns were pulled inwards from collapse of the Vierendeel trusses. There is no sign of any plane wreckage
www.youtube.com/watch?v=PgTKw1akJQQ

Chapter 11. Dark Forces: Total Destruction: Page 178

(18) Crater in WTC 6
www.whale.to/b/bollynwtc609.html

Subtitle: Evacuation and a Mystery Explosion: Page 179

(19) The Ruins of WTC 5 and WTC 6 Customs Building
www.whale.to/b/bollynwtc609.html

Subtitle: What kind of Dark Forces?: Page 181

(20) An Unusual Phenomenon
http://educate-yourself.org/lte/judywoodattacktrio13may11.shtml

(21) On-site evidence of burning heat attack
https://kendoc911.wordpress.com/debunking-dr-judy-wood/disinfo-toasted-cars/

(22) 81 St. Floor of the South Tower: Video, photos; dozens of witnesses document molten metal.
http://www.rense.com/general75/thrm.htm

Subtitle: High Order Damage: Page 187

(23) Evidence of molten slag
https://kendoc911.wordpress.com/911-molten-steel/
angle-cut/

(24) Massive girders twisted like Spaghetti
http://weburbanist.com/pics/9-11-tribute-128-photos/
attachment/5381/

(25) FBI release image of a part found near to
Murray Street
www.rense.com/general63/wtcc.htm

Chapter 12. Attack on the Pentagon: Pages 195 - 212

(26) The E4B Nightwatch or 'Flying Pentagon'
http://www.wikiwand.com/en/Boeing E-4

(27) Evidence of wreckage near the helipad at Wedge 2
https://kendoc911.wordpress.com/911-flights/
flight-77/

(28) Piece of the Fuselage with red and white letter n of American Airlines
http://www.rense.com/general31/confirm.htm

(29) White plane wreckage at Wedge 2 of West Wall
https://www.youtube.com/watch?v=4fvJ8nFa5Qk

(30) Three sources of smoke at Left, Centre explosion and Right, black smoke.
http://physics911.net/omholt/

(31) The fires were caused by the plane crash and the first major explosion.
http://wtc7.0catch.com/cars.html

(32) Removing bits of the plane
http://www.cracked.com/article_15740_was-911-inside-job.html

(33) Possible injured person but no body bags were seen to be evident.
http://pilotsfor911truth.org/forum/index.php?showtopic=22392

(34) Final collapse but edges of building are relatively smokeless with one broken window, yet cars are burnt outside the building.
https://c1.staticflickr.com/1/10/14450556_c549cc67dc.jpg

(35) Wing section of craft: Circled.
http://www.abeldanger.net/2014/04/the-list-of-innholder-thurso-wrist-that.html

(36) Four outer columns were severed prior to collapse, at pallets. The E ring sheared through the construction joints along the left side.
http://www.thenationalpatriot.com/2011/09/11/9-11-we-remember/

(37) Michael Meyer a Mechanical Engineer stated the hole was caused by shaped charges.
http://911review.org/brad.com/pentagon/exit_hole/

(38) The hole was punched out in the C ring by salvage workers after the attack.
http://www.911truth.dk/first/en/art_ExitHole.htm

(39) Command Centre (Rough Plan)
http://stevenwarran.blogspot.co.uk/2007_09_26_
archive.html

(40) Simulation of a Boeing ground level
approach at 45 degrees
http://asheepnomore.net/wp-content/uploads/2013/
12/imageee-1.jpg

(41) Final Collapse as pictured from the helipad
http://theperiledsea.ning.com/photo/american-
airlines-flight-77-8?context=location

(42) Boeing 757 allegedly hit here disappearing
at ground and first floor
http://physics911.net/omholt/

(43) Videos released by the FBI with date
recorded as 9/12 at 5pm
https://kendoc911.wordpress.com/judicial-watch-
cctv-camera/

(44) Sworn Affidavit of Special Agent Maguire
after five years

http://www.jonesreport.com/articles/071106_pentagon_video.html

(45) The real (Decoy) Flight Path over Naval Annex & Citgo Garage - Citizens Report. http://z10.invisionfree.com/Loose_Change_Forum/ar/t13778.htm

(46) Removal of a light box like section http://www.rense.com/general70/tarp.htm

(47) The removal of the plane's wing sections http://www.hoaxofthecentury.com/911PentagonStory1.htm

(48) E A3 Sky Warrior on an Aircraft Carrier - Copyright: Jeff Dyrek
navya3

(49) Pentagon: Diffuser Case http://www.911-strike.com/engines.htm

(50) Boeing 757 Diffuser Case
https://chemtrailsplanet.files.wordpress.com/2013/
02/911-pentagon-aircraft-parts.pdf

(51) A3 Diffuser Case
http://www.911-strike.com/engines.htm

(52) Pentagon: Wheel Hub
http://www.911-strike.com/engines.htm

# ACKNOWLEDGEMENTS

Barbara Lee; Cynthia McKinney; Susan Lindauer; Barbara Honegger; Sibel Edmonds; April Gallop; Bradley Manning; Carolyn Mahoney; Michael Ruppert (late); Thomas Drake; Kevin Ryan; John Lear; Ted Gunderson (late); David Ray Griffin; Alex Baker; Gordon Ross; Paul Thompson; Mike Springmann; Karl Schwarz; Richard Gage; Paul Roberts; Michel Chossudovsky; Alex Jones; Leslie Robertson; Dylan Avery; Frank De Martini; Gerard Holmgren (late); John McMurtry; Peter Dale Scott; Jeff Dyrek; Christopher Bollyn; Tom Flocco; Steven Jones; Michael Meyer; Judy Wood; Jim Fetzer; Rosalee Grable; Morgan Reynolds; Jesse Ventura; James Corbett; Kevin Barrett; Nathanial Kaplan; Barry Zwicker; Julian Assange; Edward Snowden; Devvy Kidd; Patrick Buchanan; James Mann; Dan Rather; Scott Pelley; Barry Petersen; Peter Jennings; Masudul Kabir.

# ABOUT THE AUTHOR

The writer grew up in Tamworth, Staffordshire, England. He studied Chemistry at Aston University in Birmingham and got a degree in Science from the Open University majoring in Astrophysics. He worked for 35 years as an Industrial Chemist in Applied Research in Automotive and Aerospace and as a Member of the Institute of Corrosion. He worked in the USA from 1968 to 74 constructing many of the world's largest oil storage tanks. He was in the second expedition to break the world depth record in 1962 in the Gouffre Berger in France. His first book 'Our American Hero' published in 2007 was about the death of Abraham Lincoln.

Printed in the United States
By Bookmasters